DESIRE & DECEPTION

By
Charles A. Coulombe

TOMBLAR HOUSE
Bona Tempora Volvant

Arcadia
MMIX

Printed in the United States of America

ISBN 978-0-9842365-1-0
All Rights Reserved

Desire & Deception
© Copyright 2009 by Charles A. Coulombe

Third Edition

No part of this book may be reproduced in any manner whatsoever without written permission, except in the case of brief quotations embodied in critical reviews or articles.

Published by Tumblar House
Visit our website at www.tumblarhouse.com

This book is dedicated to all of Good Will who search for the Revelation of the Truths taught by Our Lord Jesus Christ and those who have dedicated themselves to the teaching and publication of the Catholic Faith, our Pearl of Great Price—and to all those writers, ancient and modern, whose works I consulted.

We stand on the shoulders of giants.

ABOUT THE AUTHOR

Charles A. Coulombe was born in New York on 8 November 1960. At an early age, his parents took him to Hollywood, California, where they lived in an apartment building owned by famed television psychic, Criswell. Coulombe has lectured on a wide variety of historical, religious, and political topics on three continents, and did commentary for ABC News on the death of John Paul II and the election and installation of his successor. He is the author of numerous articles in many journals, and of 10 books on a variety of subjects including *Puritan's Empire*, a Catholic perspective on American history, and *Vicars of Christ*, a history of the popes.

Coulombe serves on the boards of the Queen of Angels Foundation and the Canadian Royal Heritage Trust, and is the Western United States representative of the International Monarchist League. He is or has been a member of the Knights of Columbus, the Knights of Peter Claver, the Newman Club of Los Angeles, the Mythopoeic Society, the Royal Stuart Society, and a number of others.

TABLE OF CONTENTS

PREFACE: OF PSEUDONYMS AND SMALL MINDS 1

KEEP US FROM DESOLATION 13

PHILOSOPHY IN THE EARLY CHURCH 17

BAPTISM OF DESIRE? 29

ULTRA-REALISM AND THE MIDDLE AGES 35

THE NEW PHILOSOPHY AND ST. THOMAS 45

A NEW THEOLOGY FOR A NEW WORLD 55

THE HOUND OF HELL 67

CATHOLICISM IN AMERICA 85

ATTACK ON THE DOGMA INCREASES 101

VEILED SIGN OF CONTINUITIES 109

THE FAITH CONDEMNED 125

AFTERWORD: TWENTY-FIVE YEARS LATER 143

BIBLIOGRAPHY 149

PREFACE:
OF PSEUDONYMS AND SMALL MINDS

Readers of this edition of *Desire & Deception* will notice that a major change has occurred since the last one: the name of the author. Rather than Thomas A. Hutchinson, the cover carries my moniker. The very few who follow such things will be justified in wondering why—especially since, in those far off days when this volume first saw the light, I refused to admit any part in its authorship. The reasons are somewhat complex, but interesting—not, perhaps, so much for what they might say about the book and its author, but rather about the times and places both have inhabited.

There were, in fact, two reasons why my name was not put on the first edition of this book. The first is rather straightforward: this book grew out of an editing job I did on another work (*Church of Salvation*, by Br. Leonard Mary, M.I.C.M.). It was not, at the outset, considered as an independent work.

But the second is the more exciting: it was simply because it was feared by those responsible for publishing the first edition that my writing career would suffer, due to the unpopularity of the views expressed therein. They were proved right, in the end.

The problem has been twofold: on the one hand, on the philosophical plane, I endorse herein the philosophical view variously called Christian Neo-Platonism or Ultra-Realism. Such a stand was sure to annoy the Neo-Thomists who make up a good percentage of the thinking element of more orthodox Catholics. Never mind that the Catholic creeds, liturgies, Fathers, and earlier Doctors of the Church held such views; if anything contradicted what was taught in seminary philosophy classes in 1955, it would be held by many to be anathema.

Nor would it matter if one held the same views as those ancient and venerable sources on the question of Salvation outside the

Catholic Church or the necessity of water Baptism to be saved. Again, the 50s trump all, and the older—and more authoritative—teachings were simply dismissed as *Feeneyism*. Now, of course, use of this word is generally as unfair and inaccurate as simply dismissing its users' views as *Rahnerism* would be: a usage they would rightly complain to be oversimplified. But many who consider themselves "Traditional Catholics" are quite modern in spirit, and it is a hallmark of the modern mind that it dismisses with labels anything it cannot overcome intellectually.

In any case, the elderly chap who urged a pseudonym on me was proved right by events. Rather than engaging in any sort of reasoned refutation, a number of those whose self-appointed task was the defense of an orthodoxy of their own imagining became obsessed with finding out the author's identity—the better to abuse him, as it turned out. One of these, a Catholic evangelist of some note, was sure that I was the author of the piece, and went on to harass me in a number of ways—going so far as to call a Catholic newspaper for whom I wrote to denounce me as a "Feeneyite heretic." Unfortunately for his reputation at the journal, his attempt at making an anonymous call was foiled by his speaking to an editor who had interviewed him before, and recognized his rather distinctive voice. Of course, the fact that he had stiffed the paper on advertising money he owed it did not help his cause either.

It so happened that one of his friends had decided to write an article exposing the author of *Desire & Deception* in an article in the evangelist's magazine. The friend happened to be director of catechetics for a small Midwestern diocese. Said director wrote me a letter in red ink, declaring that he was the head of a small Catholic group in his town, that he loved the book, wanted me to speak on it, but was very curious as to why my name did not appear. I did not reply (I have learned over the years not to answer letters written in colored ink, without any margins, all in capital letters, or whatever).

Nevertheless, he went ahead and wrote his sizzling expose, which predictably, was filled with ridicule but not refutation. Amused as I was, I handed over the letter to a bookstore which sold the book, so that his fulsome praise of the book could be quoted in their catalogue. It was attributed to him under his title of diocesan director of catechetics.

He called the store, outraged, the day after the catalogue appeared.

Stating his name to the lady who answered the phone (and who knew all about the article and the letter), he shouted, "Don't you know who I am?"

"Should I?"

"My name appears in your catalogue!"

"Really? Are you one of our authors?" (with great excitement).

"No! But you published my words praising that book *Desire & Deception!* I demand you remove them immediately!"

"Oh, but didn't you write them? We have the letter right here…"

"I did. But I didn't mean them!"

"Ah!" Then seamlessly gliding from ditzy to a maternal tone, she said, "I see. Well, in future, could you let us know when you're lying? Otherwise we'll presume you're telling the truth." It was an interesting riposte to an individual who was apparently outraged by my using a pseudonym.

Of course, in the Catholic world, then as now, there is nothing more untouchable, more loathsome, than a "Feeneyite." Since I have come to espouse such views, I myself have been called all sorts of things, even by close friends and family members. While this does hurt a bit, it does point up a contradiction.

Most Catholics today are really universalists—actually believing, if you analyze what they say, that almost everyone is saved, provided that they are sincere in their belief or disbelief. This is a sweeping statement to be sure, but between "Implicit Baptism of Desire" (wherein the well intentioned are part of the Church without knowing it, and so saved), Hans Urs von Balthazar's daring to hope that all men be saved, and Karl Rahner's "Anonymous Christianity" (whereby one is a member of the Church through birth, rather than Baptism), one can see little practical difference: these views cover all three major theological parties in the Church today.

Now, if what they all say is true, and sincerity is all that is required for Salvation, then by their standards I do not know a single Feeneyite who is not en route to Heaven; for there is not a single Feeneyite I have ever met who has not suffered abuse for his beliefs. If you maintain (as many writers who do not really know the topic assert) that Feeneyism is a heresy and its holders are thereby out of the Church—then what of it, since such folk hold that membership in the Church is not necessary for Salvation? Ought not Feeneyites be treated with the same decency meted out to the Patriarch of Constantinople, the Archbishop of Canterbury, the Dalai Lama, or one's own Lutheran aunt? But consistency is, after all, the bugbear of little minds.

Of course what makes it all so different today is that, when this book was written in the early 90s, one could make a juridical case against Feeneyism. Did not its holders refuse to accept the famous "decree of the Holy Office" condemning the belief back in 1949? Was not Fr. Feeney himself excommunicated for his teaching? Well, as a reading of this book will show, these were specious arguments even then. But things have changed considerably since.

Gary Potter wrote, in his 1995 book, *After the Boston Heresy Case*, (pp. 181-182) that "Ten years after the passing of Fr. Feeney, the 14 sisters of St. Ann's House were "regularized" (the word had replaced "reconciled"). That was in February 1988. Soon after, a member of Br. Francis' community in Richmond, N.H., Mr. Douglas Bersaw, wrote to Bernard Cardinal Law, Archbishop of Boston, about the regularization. Rev. John B. McCormack, Secretary for Ministerial Personnel for the Archdiocese of Boston, answered Mr. Bersaw's letter on behalf of Cardinal Law. When Mother Teresa of St. Ann's House learned of Fr. McCormack's answer, she communicated with Fr. Lawrence A. Deery, Vicar for Canonical Affairs and Judicial Vicar of the Diocese of Worcester. Fr. Deery thereupon wrote a letter to Fr. McCormack. (It is dated May 4, 1988).

> I write to clarify some aspects of the regularization which took place at St. Ann's House in Still River this past February.
> Mother Teresa, Superior of the community, has expressed concern about your letter of 7 March 1988 to Mr. Douglas Bersaw who had asked Cardinal Law for a clarification of the Church's teaching on the doctrine *extra ecclesiam nulla salus*. It is Mother Teresa's feeling that your letter implied a 'walking away' from Father Feeney's teachings on their part.
> Several clarifications might prove helpful:
> 1) The Sisters were asked to 'understand' the letter of the then Holy Office dated 8 August 1949. They were not asked to 'accept' its contents.
> 2) The Sisters were asked to make a Profession of Faith. Nothing else was required.
> It would seem that the Congregation for the Doctrine of the Faith holds the doctrine to have been defined and consequently

definitive. It is its theological interpretation and speculation which they see as problematical.

In our discussions with the Congregation it seemed rather clear that proponents of a strict interpretation of the doctrine should be given the same latitude for teaching and discussion as those who would hold more liberal views.

Summarily, Mother Teresa and her community do a great deal more than keep the memory of Father Feeney. They now actively proclaim his teachings as they did before the regularization.

I do hope this information helps to clarify the status of these Sisters and their apostolate.

St. Benedict Abbey, in Still River, which was the first group to be "regularized," on the implicit understanding that they would not preach the doctrine, nevertheless carries the three definitions on their website[1], explaining that "These days, while the document "Dominus Jesus" is a prominent issue, we at the Abbey look to the solemn definitions which the Catholic world has so frequently tried to explain, especially for the past fifty years." Br. Thomas Augustine's group, who are very staunch in upholding the "strict interpretation" of the dogma[2], were nevertheless "regularized" by the diocese in 2003, under the same understanding as St. Ann's House. Significantly, both Br. Thomas Augustine's St. Benedict Center and St. Ann's House serve as the recognized indult Mass centers for the diocese of Worcester.

It would seem obvious that the CDF do not give the 1949 letter the same importance that innumerable other commentators do (including Fr. Karl Rahner, who included it in his edition of Denzinger; since it had not existed in Latin up to that point, and did not make it into the *Acta Apostolicae Sedis* while its author was alive, Fr. Rahner was forced to translate it from English into Latin). Perhaps their superior knowledge of its actual canonical status might explain why the CDF has not demanded that the "regularized" Feeneyites "accept" it, and why nothing more was asked of Fr. Feeney in his "reconciliation" than that he recite the Athanasian Creed—which famously states the doctrine Father allowed his career to be ruined over.

---

[1] https://tinyurl.com/yaf2yuun
[2] https://tinyurl.com/y9aksxwc

The Sisters of St. Ann's House have recently published a new book, primarily of Father's lectures, entitled *Not Made For This World*. The last section is made up of anecdotes about him, the final one of which is as follows:

> The Brothers used to take Father for drives as he got older. One day, shortly before his death [i.e., 1978, six years after the "reconciliation"], they took him to the Trappist Abbey at Spencer, where the monks invited them into the cloister for lunch. Father was quiet as lunch progressed. Then he stood up, rapped his glass for attention, said, "There is no salvation outside the Catholic Church," and sat down.

Obviously, he held to his guns.

I must admit, that between Vatican II, and *Dominus Jesus*, and the *Catechism of the Catholic Church*, a great deal of confusion exists on the point; but these are all less solemn teachings than the three *ex cathedra* definitions that Feeneyites quote *ad infinitum*:

> There is but one universal Church of the faithful, outside of which no one at all is saved.
> (Pope Innocent III, Fourth Lateran Council, 1215 A.D.)

> We declare, say, define, and pronounce that it is absolutely necessary for the salvation of every human creature to be subject to the Roman Pontiff.
> (Pope Boniface VIII, the Papal Bull "Unam Sanctum", 1302 A.D.)

> The most Holy Roman Church firmly believes, professes and preaches that none of those existing outside the Catholic Church, not only pagans, but also Jews and heretics and schismatic's, can have a share in life eternal; but that they will go into the eternal fire which was prepared for the devil and his angels, unless before death they are joined with Her, and that so important is the unity of this ecclesiastical body that only those remaining within this unity can profit by the sacraments of the Church unto salvation, and they alone can receive an eternal recompense for their fasts, their almsgiving, their other works of Christian piety and the duties of a Christian soldier. No one, let his almsgiving be as great as it may, no one, not even if he pour out his blood for the Name of Christ, can be saved, unless he remain within the bosom and the unity of the Catholic Church.

Preface 7

(Pope Eugene IV, the Papal Bull "Cantate Domino", 1441 A.D.)

Now these seem about as explicit and as solemn as one can get. Had it not been for the Holy Office letter and a few generally mistranslated statements of Bl. Pius IX (in any case contradicted more or less explicitly by his Syllabus of Errors), then there really could be no question. But these more recent and less solemn documents do indeed contradict the older and more solemn ones. What is a Catholic to make of this?

A good parallel, I think, can be found in the history of the dispute over the Immaculate Conception. This has been well summarized by Fr. Alban Butler, in his *Lives of the Saints*, long before the definition of 1854 settled the issue:

> The question concerning the Immaculate Conception of the Blessed Virgin Mary had been agitated with great warmth in the university of Paris, when both the University and the bishop, in 1387, condemned certain propositions of John de Montesano, a Dominican, in which this privilege was denied. The Council of Basel, in 1439 (Sess. 36), declared the belief of her Immaculate Conception to be conformable to the doctrine and devotion of the church, to the Catholic faith, right reason, and the holy scriptures, and to be held by all Catholics. But this council was at that time a schismatical assembly, nor could its decree be of force. It was, nevertheless, received by a provincial council held at Avignon in 1457, and by the university of Paris. When some gave scandal by warmly contesting the Immaculate Conception, this famous university passed a decree in 1497, in which it was enacted, that no one should be admitted in it to the degree of doctor of divinity who did not bind himself by oath to defend this point. (See Spondan, Contin. Baron. Ad an. 1497; Bulaeus, Hist. Universit. Paris, t. 5, p. 815; Fleury, cont. t. 24, p. 336; Frassen, t. 8, p. 227). The council of Trent declared, in the decree concerning original sin, that it was not its intention to include in it the Immaculate Virgin, the Mother of God, and ordered the decree of Sixtus IV, relating to this point, to be observed. That pope, in 1476, granted certain indulgences to those who assisted at the office and mass on the feast of her Conception; and, in 1483, by another constitution, forbade anyone to censure this festival, or to condemn the opinion which asserted the Virgin Mary's Immaculate Conception. St. Pius V, by his bull in 1570, forbade either the opinion which affirmed, or that which denied it, to be

censured. Paul V, in 1616, reiterated the same prohibition, and, in 1617, forbade anyone to affirm in sermons, theses, or other like public acts, that the Blessed Virgin Mary was conceived in original sin. Gregory XV, in 1622, forbade anyone to affirm this, even in private disputations, except those to whom the holy see gives a special license to do it, which he granted to the Dominicans, provided they do it privately, and only among themselves [emphasis added]; but he ordered that, in the office or mass of this festival, no other title than simply that of the Conception should be used. Alexander VII, in 1671, declared that the devotion of honoring the Immaculate Conception of the Virgin Mary is pious; yet prohibits censuring those who do not believe her Conception immaculate. Philip III of Spain, demanded of Paul V, and Philip IV, of Gregory XV, a definition of this question, but could obtain nothing more than the foregoing bulls. (See Luke Wadding, the learned Irish Franciscan, who lived some time in Spain, and died at Rome in 1655, De Legatione Philippi III et Philippi IV ad Paulum V et Greg. XV, pro definienda Controversia de Conceptione Virginis). In the latest edition of the Roman Index, a certain little office of the Immaculate Conception is condemned; but this censure is not to be extended to other such little offices. In the prayers themselves it is called the Conception of the Immaculate Virgin, which phrase is ambiguous, and may be understood to imply only that she was spotless from all actual sin, and was cleansed from original sin before she was born, in which all Catholics agree. Benedict XIII granted to the subjects of Austria, and the empire a weekly office of the Immaculate Conception on every Saturday; but the epithet Immaculate Conception occurs not in any of the prayers, but only in the title of the office. This prudent reserve of the church in her public prayers is a caution to her children, whilst they maintain this pious sentiment, not to exceed the bounds which she has prescribed them [emphasis mine]; though certain devotions are used in many parts, in which the Conception is called immaculate in the prayers themselves. It is the mystery of the Immaculation, or Sanctification of the Blessed Virgin Mary, which is the object of the devotion of the church on this festival, rather than her bare Conception... (Butler, *op. cit.* vol. IV p. 493)

Of course, as we know now, Fr. Butler's final explanation of the feast was erroneous; but he had plenty of reason to be wrong. St. Thomas Aquinas had denied the Immaculate Conception in the *Summa*, and had not the Fathers of Trent had the Summa placed upon the altar during their deliberations? (Of course, since 1854, all imprimatured editions of the *Summa* without correctives on this point have carried defective approbations). The note of caution Fr. Butler sounds in the penultimate sentence may well have been directed toward such of his contemporaries as Charles III of Spain, who ordered all his civil servants to swear an oath to defend the Immaculate Conception to the death (His Most Catholic Majesty's contradictory nature may be evoked by reflecting both upon his financing of St. Junipero Serra in California, and his expulsion of the Jesuits from the Spanish domains). Against St. Thomas, there were simply the University of Paris, the schismatic Council of Basel, and the Lullists and Scotists. While not wanting to endorse Basel, I think that the much put-upon University and the Franciscan philosophers, so often slandered on this very point from the 13th to 19th centuries, deserve an enormous apology.

We are, of course, in a Pontificate as much concerned with theological change (as were the immediately preceding ones) as with clarity (this a welcome alteration). As a result, Benedict XVI has apparently set about resolving contradictions. Thus, in his Christmas message to the Curia he boldly addressed the differences between the documents of Vatican II and the Syllabus of Errors. His resolution of the issue is to declare that no solemn or infallible truths are covered by either set of decrees, but are both contingent upon real-world conditions. If he is correct, then that means that the former may be as vigorously questioned as the latter has been so completely forgotten. His Holiness opened up an enquiry into Limbo, which many confidently predicted would lead to this teaching being set aside (such as Fr. Richard McBrien happily pointing out that this will doom Original Sin). In the event, the document produced by the International Theological Commission was forgotten as soon as it came out.

Why? Because the men who produced the document, although wanting to allow Limbo to be set aside, were honest scholars and historians. The first half of the piece accurately describes the development of doctrine on Limbo, and shows that it was indeed, indisputably, the common teaching of the Church until, in the words of the document: "In the 20th century, however, theologians sought the right to imagine new solutions, including the possibility that Christ's full salvation reaches these infants." The rest of the document attempts to justify these imaginings—and, if one is candid and a believer in immutable truth, falls exceedingly flat. It is no surprise that it was forgotten by those who had trumpeted it as soon as it was released and read.

Fr. Feeney was, in reality, a peripheral member of the *Ressourcement*, the theological movement among many Jesuits and Dominicans in the mid-20th century to return for inspiration to the Church Fathers and the Doctors of the Church other than St. Thomas Aquinas. What these diverse *Ressourceurs* had in common was the view that for many Catholics the Faith had become an intellectual or cultural abstraction, rather than something to redeem and transform their lives. The solution to this problem, they believed, lay in a return to the sources—and this solution was often invoked at Vatican II. The problem, of course, was that such a return negates many of the comfortable compromises that have allowed Catholics to live in a society that has more or less despised them for several centuries. Many of Fr. Feeney's colleagues found a way out of this by relativizing the Fathers, Doctors, and Solemn teachings of Popes and Councils in such a way as to make them palatable to modern sensibilities (including their own). Fr. Feeney chose to take them at face value—in the way which their authors intended them to be taken. He suffered the consequences of such a stand.

I do not believe, humanly speaking, that an authoritative definition on *extra ecclesiam nulla salus* reaffirming the three cited definitions is likely to happen anytime soon. Rather, I believe that, as with the Immaculate Conception, they will be affirmed whenever the Holy Ghost decides. As has been pointed out to me, the "Feeney/SBC position" "was essentially that assumed to be true by millions of Catholics for many centuries." Indeed it was. And what Catholics they were: the Fathers, the Doctors, and all the great Missionaries like St. Francis Xavier, to say nothing of those three annoying definitions.

Against all that, I am supposed to side with the more "advanced" theologians of the 19th and early 20th centuries, almost all those of the past five decades, and a handful of less solemn documents, whose place in the Magisterium is at least questionable. Those who held the "Feeney/SBC" position built up the Church; those who opposed it have produced what we have. If I am to take Our Lord at face value, then by their fruits, at least, I will know them. It is the abiding presence of the Holy Ghost with His Church, despite all that we churchmen do to frustrate the truth, that has thus far prevented the Magisterium from solemnly defining against the doctrine EENS, even as it prevented it from endorsing the Thomistic denial of the Immaculate Conception.

And so, all "proponents of a strict interpretation of the doctrine," must, in keeping with the CDF's advice to the Diocese of Worcester "be given the same latitude for teaching and discussion as those who would hold more liberal views." Rome has spoken, to be sure; but the case is not yet closed. In any case, I would hope that the ideas in this book will be debated, rather than the author attacked for thinking them—in a word, that the need for pseudonyms has passed. After all, if, in a debate, one of the parties sinks down to the *ad hominem*, he declares that he has lost the argument.

 Charles A. Coulombe
 Arcadia, California
 24 September 2009
 Our Lady of Ransom

KEEP US FROM DESOLATION

The Catholic Church is sick in head and members. This can only be doubted by the deaf, the dumb, the blind—and those with a vested interested in the present decline. The evidences of that decline in terms of regular communicants, vocations, education, liturgy, and so on have been chronicled admirably by many other writers, and this writer feels no need to add to those chronicles. Rather, he would prefer to shed light on one factor in that decline.

It is true that diverse reasons may be adduced for the present malaise. Liturgically, the alterations made in the past several decades have had disastrous results, to be sure; coupled with these have been an unending flow of theological stupidities from experts and bishops alike. The twin heresies of Americanism and Modernism (the former being the official creed of the single most wealthy and powerful segment of the Church long before Vatican II) may be seen as the proximate causes, certainly. Others have pointed out such things as the pre-Vatican II undue adulation of clerics, which prepared the Catholic faithful to accept anything one said—regardless of its veracity—so long as the one in question wore a Roman collar. Still others would point to various political and economic factors. While all these mentioned played their part, of a certainty, it is my considered belief that history reveals an ultimate source of the present mess. Had this source not been present, all the other items enumerated could not have had the devastating effects they did have upon us. What, then, is this ultimate source?

We must return to the first principles, to the reason for being of the Church. If a Catholic is asked why he is one, these days he is likely to give all sorts of answers: "I was raised that way." That is little help, indeed. What if you had been raised a Nazi? "Well, historically, it is the Church Christ founded." Better, but so what? Christ founded a Church, Buddha a way of supposedly escaping the pain of life, Mohammed a way of surrender to the Will of Allah. So what? Why be Catholic? The answer is simple. Because the Church is the means God has ordained for every human being to save his or her soul.

You may recall the old saying "In Adam's Fall, we sinned all." Prior to Christ's coming, so the Church teaches, no one achieved Salvation; that is, none received after death the Beatific Vision and eternal union with God in Heaven. The wicked went, of course, to Hell, but even the Just languished in the "Limbo of the Fathers," barred from Heaven by their fallen human nature. To rescue us from Hell, Christ was born and set up the Sacraments and the Church which dispenses them. Christ described the problem in rather stark terms:

> Lord, are they few that are saved? But He said to them: Strive to enter by the narrow gate; for many, I say to you, shall seek to enter, and shall not be able. (Luke 13:23, 24)

> Enter ye in at the narrow gate: for wide is the gate and broad is the way that leadeth to destruction, and many there are who go in thereat. How narrow is the gate and how strait the way that leadeth to life, and few there are who find it! (Matthew 7:13, 14)

Rather a negative attitude, we would say today! But actually, given the facts of fallen nature, merely realistic. It would really have been dreadful if He had not prescribed a solution. Providentially, He did:

> Amen, Amen, I say to you, unless a man be born again of water and the Holy Ghost, he cannot enter into the kingdom of God. (John 3:5)

> He that believeth and is baptized, shall be saved; but he that believeth not shall be condemned. (Mark 16:16)

> I am the living bread which came down from heaven.
> If any man eat of this bread, he shall live forever; and the bread that I will give, is my flesh, for the life of the world.
> The Jews therefore strove among themselves, saying: How can this man give us his flesh to eat?
> Then Jesus said to them: Amen, amen, I say unto you: Except you eat the flesh of the Son of man, and drink his blood, you shall not have life in you. He that eateth my flesh and drinketh my blood, hath everlasting life: and I will raise him up on the last day.

Keep Us From Desolation 15

    For my flesh is meat indeed: and my blood is drink indeed. He that eateth my flesh and drinketh my blood, abideth in me, and I in him.
    As the living Father hath sent me, and I live by the Father: so he that eateth me, the same shall also live by me. (John 6:51-58)

    Jesus said to him: "Thou art Peter; and upon this rock I will build my church, and the gates of hell shall not prevail against it. And I will give to thee the keys of the kingdom of heaven.
    And whatsoever thou shalt bind upon earth, it shall be bound also in heaven; and whatsoever thou shalt loose on earth, it shall be loosed also in heaven. (Matthew 16:18-19)

    Going therefore teach ye all nations: baptizing them in the name of the Father, and of the Son, and of the Holy Ghost. Teaching them to observe all things whatsoever I have commanded you: and behold I am with you all days even to the consummation of the world. (Matthew 28:19-20)

    He that heareth you, heareth Me; and he that despiseth you, despiseth Me. (Luke 10:16)

    One could quote other texts, but in these you see Christ's answer to the problem of the Fall. The sacraments are the means; the Church dispenses them; her head, successor to Peter, wields the power of the keys and administers the Church; her members are to spread it all over the world, and He will be with them; lastly, acceptance or rejection of that Church is the equivalent of similar action toward Him. He offers no other way to escape the trap of being human.
    So it was then. Today, apparently, things are different! *Commonweal* is a magazine which for long decades has been the voice of intellectual American Catholicism. In its pages one will find advertisements for such things as Paulist Press' newest book releases, the Ph.D. program at Loyola University of Chicago, Theology and Pastoral Ministry Graduate Studies at the University of Dayton, and Graduate Studies in Theology at Boston College (prestigious Catholic schools all). In a word, *Commonweal* is written, supported, and read by the dominant set in the American Church, itself (at least financially) the dominant segment in the Church Universal. The 17 January 1992 issue carried on the back cover, as a subscription appeal sample, a Dore engraving of Hell.

Next to it, under the catchy slogan DAMNATION JUST ISN'T WHAT IT USED TO BE, is an excerpt from an article by Paul Elie run in the 27 September 1991 issue and entitled *On Young Catholics and the Church*:

> Current discussions about young Catholics suggest that Catholic leaders are less concerned with our welfare than with the well-being of the church general. This is a natural consequence of the Second Vatican Council's revised understanding of the church, and its corresponding revision of the nature of salvation. If you see the church chiefly as the body of its people, and not chiefly, as, say, a divine agency appointed by God to do his saving work on earth, your in-house evangelizing efforts will be less menacing but also somewhat less compelling ... Your sense that Catholicism isn't taking hold on the younger end leads you to think not of souls lost for eternity, but of the church losing its vigor in the here and now. Because you can't get all worked up about young people going to hell, you mostly worry that if you fail to sponsor a Catholic identity in them, the religion you've known will go out of this corner of the world, and the kids will have missed something grand.

If what Mr. Elie says is true, then the Church is not something grand; she is something worthless; a fundraiser for parasites based upon a 2000-year-old swindle. Why indeed should young folk have anything to do with that? As we have just seen, Christ's vision of the Church was precisely that "of a divine agency appointed by God to do his saving work on earth." If she were merely the "body of its people," then judging by both its history and its present state, she is a pitiful thing which ought to be put out of her misery post-haste. The fact that the *Commonweal* gang would consider a piece like this an inducement to subscribe tells us much about the mindset of many in the ruling circles of the Church.

Contrary, however, to what Mr. Elie says, this change is not to be laid entirely at the feet of Vatican II (although there can be no doubt that "believers" of this stripe can find justification in its ambiguous documents). No, it has been "a long, long trail a-winding" from the clear teaching on the Church as enunciated by Christ, through twenty centuries to the near complete dominance of opposite ideas. We shall dip into the current of Church history and teaching to see how this alteration came about, and whether it was justified.

PHILOSOPHY IN THE EARLY CHURCH

Christ's view of the Church as sole means of Salvation via the Sacraments was continued during the Apostolic Age. In his first letter to the Corinthians (4:4), St. Paul informed them: "For I have nothing on my conscience, yet I am not thereby justified." Mere clearness of conscience, it was agreed, was not enough to rescue the individual from the curse of Adam's seed. The change wrought by Baptism and the reception of the other sacraments were required to save one from the eventual doom lying in wait for natural, fallen Man, and indeed, all fallen nature. The most frequent simile used to illustrate the saving methods of the Church (and her absolute necessity) was that first broached by St. Peter in his first epistle (3:20-21): "In the days of Noah, when the ark was a-building, eight souls were saved by water. Whereunto Baptism, being of like form, now saveth you also."

As was said before, no one went to Heaven prior to the Ascension of Jesus; not the Just of the Old Testament nor anyone else. (Enoch and Elias did not die but were taken away from among men in the flesh.) But those who were justified (lived by the natural law in expectation of the coming of the Messiah) were neither punished for sins, nor to be in Limbo forever. They (and their number included St. Dismas the Good Thief) were liberated from their prison by Christ, and ascended with Him 40 days after the Resurrection, as Cornelius à Lapide tells us.

At this point, it were well to indicate that, while the Old Dispensation, which we have just looked at, and the New Dispensation (requiring the Sacraments) were very different, there were significant links between them. But we must look at a few philosophical concepts to grasp them adequately.

The Church Fathers looked primarily to Plato as the foremost Greek philosopher. He first proposed the idea of "Universals," that is of ideal prototypes of things like "Man" and "Horse," as well as abstract qualities like "Love" and "Honor." These Plato held to exist in some "realm of the Types" whence they cast reflections on our poor earth. We ourselves, for instance, are mere reflections of the great archetype "Man," of whose substance we all partake—hence our "mannishness."

Now these concepts were synthesized philosophically with Judaism by such as Philo of Alexandria. Christian philosophers deduced that these "types" did not exist in some kingdom of their own, but in the mind of God. They were no less real for all of that; in a certain sense they were more real than those of their reflections which were soulless (rocks, etc.). Further, these archetypes share the timelessness of God—for He has thought of them for all eternity. So applying this idea to the Old Testament, they found, that just as the Holy Ghost—the *Shekinah*, pillar of fire by night, cloud by day, and presence in the Ark of the Covenant—had existed from all eternity (although His early manifestation was first clearly seen in the Baptism at the Jordan, and then at Pentecost), so too had the Son, the divine *Logos* although not yet incarnate. Similarly, from all eternity was Our Lady, the vessel whereby the Logos became flesh, present in the mind of God as the figure of Wisdom, of *Sophia*. In the same manner, all those Just who had lived under the Old Law (the Patriarchs of the Old Testament, to whom many added such gentiles whose writings or sayings apparently indicated they too were waiting for the Messiah—Socrates, Virgil, Plato, etc.), since they would be inserted into the Church Triumphant after the Ascension, were held to be part of the Church—as was, in a prefiguring sense, the Jewish Temple. "And no man hath ascended into heaven, but he that descended from heaven, the Son of Man who is in heaven (John 3:13)." So the Church was held to have always existed as the Mystical Body of Christ in the mind of God. You may recall what is implied in the Gospel about time being, with space, a part of Creation, and so not really experienced by God, who is outside His Creation: "Before Abraham was, I am," as Christ said. This view of time from God's point of view was held by the Fathers, and must be borne in mind with what has just been said about the Universals, in order to make sense of the views on Salvation of the Church Fathers.

For it was in this sense that Pope St. Clement I included in his letter to the Corinthians:

Philosophy in the Early Church

> Let us go through all generations and learn that in generation to generation the Master has given a place of repentance to those willing to turn to Him. Noah preached repentance, and those who heard him were saved. Jonah preached repentance to the Ninivites; those who repented for their sins appeased God in praying, and received salvation, even though they were aliens of God. (1 Clement 7:5-1)

Obviously, the salvific work of the Church, carried on by the prophets before Christ, could receive its full fruition only after Christ came. The salvation referred to here was that physical salvation which kept the City of Nineveh from immediate ruin; though it may be that some of those Ninivites came also to share in Jonah's expectation of the Messiah, and so perhaps of his eventual ransoming from Limbo.

Here too we see suggested another Platonic concept: the primacy of the Will over the Intellect. The Will, according to Plato and those, Christians or otherwise, who follow him, is the basic motive force of the personality. It is oriented at any given time to Love of Truth and Love of Self in varying proportions. The Intellect, that faculty which perceives and interprets outer phenomena (whether through learning or sense) is formed and steered as it were by the Will, and accordingly forms impressions depending on whether the Will is more oriented toward love of Truth or love of Self. So two pagans, faced with the Faith, will react differently. The one, motivated to a greater or lesser degree by love of Truth, responds immediately or gradually to the Faith, thereby embracing it despite whatever kind of unpleasantness or personal renunciations might be necessary to do so. The other, whose Will is dominated by love of Self, and reacting strictly in terms of what will please or convenience him (either personally or by means of kindred, etc.), rejects the Faith. Yet both are equipped with roughly equal intellects.

In both Dispensations, God did and does respond to Good Will with the Faith: whether, as in the Old Law with the Ninivites, by means of Jonah, or in the New, as He dealt with the eunuch of the Ethiopian Queen:

> Now an angel of the Lord spoke to Philip, saying: Arise, go towards the south, to the way that goeth down from Jerusalem into Gaza: this is desert.

> And rising up he went. And behold a man of Ethiopia, a eunuch, of great authority under Candace the queen of the Ethiopians, who had charge over all of her treasures, had come to Jerusalem to adore.
> And he was returning, sitting in his chariot, and reading Isaias the prophet.
> And the Spirit said to Philip: Go near, and join thyself to this chariot.
> And Philip running thither, heard him reading the prophet Isaias. And he said: Thinkest thou that thou understandest what thou readest?
> Who said: And how can I, unless some man shew me? And he desired Philip that he would come up and sit with him.
> And the piece of scripture which he was reading was this: He was led as a sheep to the slaughter; and like a lamb without voice before his shearer, so openeth he not his mouth.
> In humility his judgment was taken away. His generation who shall declare for his life shall be taken from the earth?
> And the eunuch answering Philip said: I beseech thee, of whom doth the prophet speak this? Of himself, or of some other man?
> Then Philip, opening his mouth, and beginning at this scripture, preached unto him Jesus.
> And as they went on their way, they came to a certain water; and the eunuch said: See, here is water; what doth hinder me from being baptized?
> And Philip said: If thou believest with all thy heart, thou mayest. And he answering, said: I believe that Jesus Christ is the Son of God.
> And he commanded the chariot to stand still; and they went down into the water, both Philip and the eunuch: and he baptized him.
> And when they were come up out of the water, the Spirit of the Lord took away Philip; and the eunuch saw him no more. And he went on his way rejoicing. (Acts 8:26-39)

Here we see the working of Grace upon free will. For the eunuch loved truth, as shown by his making the long trip to Jerusalem and studying Isaiah on his own; God rewards his good will by sending Philip. It is interesting also that, by more conventional non-miraculous means, Philip spent the first part of the chapter evangelizing the Samaritans. After he leaves the eunuch, he goes back to that kind of work. So the faith will be brought to the good-willed either by miraculous or conventional means.

It is important to understand also that, for the early Church, Good Will was seen as a part of the working of Christ drawing men into His Church. Putting together all the ideas we have been discussing, let us see what various Fathers have to say with regard to the eternity of the Church as the Mystical Body of Christ, the membership of the good-willed of the old dispensation in it, and the ultimate origin in Christ, the Logos, of all Good Will.

St. Justin Martyr (100-165) was one of the earliest apologists. In his *First Apology* (cap 46), he says:

> Christ is the Logos of whom the whole race of men partake. Those who lived according to Logos are Christians, even if they were considered atheists *[meaning, in classical times, monotheists who disbelieved in the gods of mythology]*, such as, among the Greeks, Socrates and Heraclitus.

Here we see at once that a) Christ's salvation has always been available; b) those in the past of Good Will ("who *lived* according to the Logos") *are* members of the Church—this because of their incorporation into Christ's Mystical Body at the time of His Descent into Hell (Limbo), even as we recite in the Creed. Notice Justin's juxtaposition of "lived" and "are" (reflecting God's sense of time). Socrates (et al.) *were* "just" men under the Old Law, and so *are* members of the Church now—the Church Triumphant—as a result of the Descent and Ascension of Christ and his own incorporation into Him.

The second Century work, *The Shepherd of Hermas*, (brother of Pope St. Pius I) includes (in Vision 2.4.1) an account of Hermas' being asked by an angel who he believes the old woman to be who had given him a little book. He replies that it is the Sibyl. The angel says: "You are wrong... It is the Church. Who said to him: why an old woman? He said: Because she was created first of all; for this reason she is an old woman, and because of her the world was established." Like Our Lady, the Lady Ecclesia had always been in the Mind of God, and so had always been real. But just as the Logos Incarnate was Christ, and Wisdom incarnate was the Blessed Virgin, Mother of the Church, so too did the ideal of the Church take flesh, in a sense, at the establishment of the Church at the first Pentecost.

This idea is repeated in the second letter of Pope St. Clement I to the Corinthians (14.2): "The books of the prophets and the apostles [say] that the Church is not [only] now, but from the beginning. She was manifested in the last days to save us." It was impossible to understand his sentiment, unless one realize the acceptance by the Church Fathers of the Platonic view of Universals.

St. Irenaeus also bears witness to both the differences in the Old Law between Jews and Gentiles, and between the Old Law and the New:

> There is one and the same God the Father and His Logos, always assisting the human race, with varied arrangement to be sure, and doing many things, and saving from the beginning those who are saved, for they are those who love God, and, according to their age follow His Logos (*Against Heresies*, 4.28.2)

There is one set of rules for Salvation under the Old Law, and another under the New. In the same vein, he tells us:

> Christ came not only for those who believed in the time of Tiberius Caesar, nor did the Father provide only for those who are now, but for absolutely all men from the beginning, who according to their ability, feared and loved God and lived justly... and desired to see Christ and to hear His voice (op. cit., 4.22.2).

Such a one was Virgil supposed to be, who longed in his fourth *Eclogue* for the child who was to "rule with his father's virtues the world at peace."

Nor was St. Clement of Alexandria reluctant to speak of the economy of Salvation prior to the Incarnation:

> From what has been said, I think it is clear that there is but one true Church, which is really ancient, into which those who are just according to design are enrolled. (*Stromate* 7.17, Migne, *Patrologia Graeca* IX, p.992).

In the same work he voices such sentiments as, "Before the coming of the Lord, philosophy was necessary for justification to the Greeks; now it is useful for piety... for it brought the Greeks to Christ as the Law did the Hebrews" (1.5); and "To the one he gave the commandments, to the others philosophy, with the result that everyone who did not believe was without excuse" (7.2). Of course, St. Clement believed that Plato derived much of his teaching from the Jews in any case. But being antagonistic toward much of the rest of Greek philosophy, he also held that, as Platonic philosophy was as much a preparation for the Gospel as Judaism, neither race in God's providence had any excuse for rejecting Christianity. Indeed, as "the soul is naturally Christian" (in the words of Tertullian, St. Clement's opposite in philosophy, personality, etc.), later missionary experience has shown that every culture has some "preparation for the Gospel."

> Origen, St. Clement's great pupil, was just as Platonic. Do not think I speak of the spouse or the church [only] from the coming of the Saviour in the flesh, but from the beginning of the human race, in fact, to seek out the origin of this mystery more deeply with Paul as leader, even before the foundation of the world. (Migne, *Patrologia Graeca*, XIII, 134).

But while, prior to their respective incarnation, the Logos, Holy Wisdom, and the Church acted and worked in an invisible manner, afterwards Christ, Our Lady and the Church were visible and active. Similarly, while in the Old Dispensation the Just could be connected to them in a wholly spiritual manner, the Just of the New required visible connections. From vague potentialities and future promises, the mechanics of Salvation became fully enfleshed; the more so because it was not incorporation into Christ after Death that was involved, but during life through Church and Sacraments.

So it is that Hermas says in *The Shepherd* (*Similtudes*, 9.16):

> These apostles and the teachers who preached the name of the Son of God, when they fell asleep in the power and faith of the Son of God, preached also to those who had fallen asleep earlier, and they gave them the seal of the preaching. They therefore went down into the water with them, and came up again.

This bears reference to the manner in which the liberated from Limbo were incorporated into Christ.

St. Justin Martyr says in his *First Apology* (cap. 46):

> Then they [the newly converted] are led by us where there is water, and are regenerated... For Christ said: Unless you are born again, you will not enter into the kingdom of heaven.

Whatever the case before Christ's advent, this is the way now. The Universal "Man" having fallen in its two earthly expressions, Adam and Eve, all who partake of its substance, must be made into new creatures, must take on the Divine Nature and become members of Christ.

About 180, St. Theophilus of Antioch wrote in his letter *To Autolycus*: "God has given the world a holy Church in whose safe harbor the lovers of truth seek refuge, as well as those who desire to be saved and to escape the dreadful wrath of God."

St. Justin Martyr's most obvious philosophical successor, St. Clement of Alexandria, writes in the *Stromata* (5.12, Migne, *Patrologia Graeca*, IX, 128): "He who does not enter through the door is a thief and a robber... Therefore it is necessary for them to learn the truth through Christ and be saved, even if they happen on philosophy." What once could be a justifying preparation for the Gospel is, under the New Law, no longer sufficient for Salvation "...the will of God is man's salvation, and this will is called the Church, which consists of those whom God called and saved" (*The Pedagogue*, Bk 1, Migne, *Patrologia Graeca*, VIII).

Nor is Origen silent:

> If anyone from this people wants to be saved, let him come to this house, that he might attain salvation; let him come into this house, in which is the Blood of Christ in sign of redemption... Let no one therefore persuade himself, let no one deceive himself: outside of this house, that is outside of the Church, no one is saved; for, if anyone should go out of it, he is guilty of his own death. (*In Jesu Nave homilae*, III, n. 5, Migne, *Patrologia Graeca*, IX, 129).

His *In Josue* (III, Migne, *Patrologia Graeca*, 825) contrasts the Church to the heresies that were already roaming about: "The distinctive mark of the Catholic is to belong to the Church outside of which there is no salvation. On the contrary, he who leaves the Church walks in darkness: he is a heretic." "It is not possible to receive forgiveness of sins without Baptism," he opines in his *Exhortation to the Martyrs*. Incidentally, these and similar statements give the lie to the often-repeated charge that Origen believed in the eventual redemption of all, including Satan. It is true that he speaks of a final consummation; but, given his other opinions, that may easily be squared with eternal damnation. Some of his disciples on the other hand certainly held various of the condemned ideas he has been charged with; presumably they were eager to associate the master with their own beliefs.

It is hardly necessary to cite St. Cyprian, to whom we owe the pithy formula "Outside the Church there is no Salvation." We could go on and on, citing Church Fathers, but it should be obvious that, for the Fathers, Christ's view of the work of the Church still held good.

In subsequent ages, the Platonic (or Ultra-Realist, from its insistence on the actual reality of the Universals in the mind of God) view of things came to be superseded by other philosophies. Working backward from their own points-of-view, later theologians and scholars came to believe (for reasons we will look at later) that references in the writings of the Fathers to conditions under the Old Law were actually applicable to non-Christians in remote areas under the New. This is an erroneous, but nevertheless widespread view.

Proof of the actual contemporary teaching in the age of the Fathers may be found in the Creed of St. Athanasius, accepted by the Church alongside the Apostles' and the Nicene Creeds. In its beginning and ending we see the distillation of the orthodox Faith at the time of the Arian heresy. It commences: "Whoever wants to be saved must, before all other things, hold the Catholic Faith, which unless one preserves integral and inviolate, without doubt he will perish eternally." After treating at length about the Trinity, this Creed ends: "This is the Catholic Faith which, unless one faithfully and firmly believes, he cannot be saved."

Similarly, a cursory reading of the *Roman Martyrology* reveals a small number of martyred catechumens who, despite having apparently been put to death for the Faith without Baptism, were accounted Saints in Heaven. To account for this supposed discrepancy, even some few of the later Church Fathers came to believe in a theory of "baptism of blood"; that is, that those who died unbaptized for the Faith somehow partook of the graces of Baptism, of the regeneration of the soul which takes place therein.

This was doubtless suggested by the fact that martyrdom was indeed held to absolve the Baptized of all unconfessed sins.

Certainly, it is a notion which has no scriptural foundation: if one looks further, it would certainly have found no place among the Ultra-Realist early Church Fathers to whom one's own fallen blood, sprung of Adam, simply could not have the salvific effects of Christ's Precious Blood, which is applied to the individual soul through the waters of Baptism. If it did, why would Christ have come? Nor could a Platonist figure how something human would be able to perform such a task not in keeping with its nature.

Further, the accounts in the *Martyrology* for the most part speak of those catechumens imprisoned for a time prior to execution. But we know that it was the rule for Christians in prison to be baptized soon upon entrance therein to prepare them for death; it is from such accounts, for example, that we know that infants were baptized, although outside of jail baptism was generally deferred until adulthood. Also, the word "catechumen" did not always refer to the unbaptized. As St. Ambrose told his own Catechumen class:

> I know very well that many things still have to be explained. It may strike you as strange that you were not given a complete teaching *before you were baptized.* However, the ancient discipline of the Church forbids us to reveal the mysteries to the uninitiated. (*De Mysteriis*).

The two most frequently cited accounts of supposed "baptisms of blood" are those of St. Emerentiana (23 January), and a soldier martyred with St. Alban (22 June). The first named was "stoned by the heathens while still a catechumen…" But she was moreover a *Phtizomenoi*— "One coming into the light." If she had truly not been baptized, it must be expected that someone would have done so while she lay dying. As far as the soldier companion of St. Alban is concerned, it is rather a garbled account. He was accompanying St. Alban to the latter's execution, and was converted on the spot, desiring to die with the saint. At the top of the hill where the deed was to be executed, a spring burst forth at St. Alban's prayer. While St. Bede in his account of the occurrence claims that the soldier "had not been cleansed in the water of baptism, but he was cleansed by the outpouring of his own blood," he also says just prior to this, concerning the miraculous spring, "the river, its sacred office fulfilled, returned obediently to its spot." One cannot help wondering just what that sacred office was, why St. Alban figured it necessary to pray for it, and whether St. Bede, writing about four centuries after the fact, using ancient documents, didn't miss something. Accounts of martyrs are hardly infallible documents.

Even the phrase, "baptized in blood," sounds suspiciously like a mere turn of phrase. Centuries later, during the Holy Wars against the Muslims, Crusaders were often spoken of as being "baptized in Turk's blood." One cringes to think of the theological implications of a literal reading of that! That it was in fact an idiomatic, rather than a doctrinal statement is borne out by St. John Damascene (*Barlaam and Josaphat*, Woodward & Heineman, trans., pp. 169-171):

> These things were well understood by our holy and inspired fathers—thus they strove, after Holy Baptism, to keep… spotless and undefiled. Whence some of them also thought fit to receive yet another Baptism: I mean that which is by blood and martyrdom.

Therefore, "baptism of blood" appeared to have been a common description of the martyrdom of a baptized Catholic. At any rate, the erroneous interpretation appears (as we shall see) to have been condemned at the Council of Florence.

BAPTISM OF DESIRE?

A similar concept, "baptism of desire," seems to owe its genesis to flawed reading of a sermon of St. Ambrose, the famed and much quoted *Oration on Valentinian*. Valentinian II, young and much beloved Emperor of the West, who had been Ambrose's ward in childhood, appealed to Ambrose to baptize him while the youthful Emperor was in Gaul. Before this could happen, Valentinian was killed in rather mysterious circumstances (not fully explained even today) by a usurping military commander who held the preponderance of power in the province. The body was brought back to Milan for burial, and St. Ambrose delivered a sermon to the mourners; Valentinian's sister and mother sat in the front row. It was a tense situation indeed, as Fr. Fernand Mourret, S.S. informs us:

> At the funeral of the prince, the Church must make her voice heard. Ambrose was appointed to be its interpreter. How would he acquit himself? The people were expecting an expression of their grief and of their indignation. And assuredly, he shared in both of these feelings. But how was he to give voice to such feelings without pointing out and cursing the hand that had struck in the dark? "Never did oratorical art face a more delicate task and emerge more happily." What deep and restrained feeling there is in these words of the exordium: "Valentinian comes back to us, but not as we hoped to see him return. Upon hearing that the Alps were threatened by barbarians, he resolved to come and share our dangers. He fell, struck down by death, at his first steps in public life. I refer to the suddenness of his death, not to its manner, for I weep and do not accuse... How much better it would be for bishops to be persecuted by the emperors than to be loved by them. I was happier when I was the one risking my life for my prince than now when I must lament his death." For a whole hour the preacher kept an immense throng hanging on his words. The anxious and deeply affected people made him understand that their soul vibrated with his, although in his sermon not an

offensive word could be found against the new ruler. (Mourett, Fernand, N. Thompson, trans., *A History of the Catholic Church*, II, 406).

Doubtless it was a masterpiece of its kind, and performed its political purpose adequately. But he uttered in the course of his sermon three fateful sentences, upon which a whole structure of thought has since been built up. As Valentinian had not, to public knowledge, been baptized before his death, his soul was despaired of by many. But in the highly charged atmosphere of grief, fear, and popular anger surrounding the funeral, St. Ambrose said: "Did he not obtain the grace which he desired? Did he not obtain what he asked for? Certainly he obtained it, because he asked for it." Very many people throughout the centuries, his own disciple St. Augustine included, have taken those three terse lines to mean that St. Ambrose believed that Valentinian had been saved without actually passing through the waters of Baptism.

But in fact, this is an incorrect interpretation of St. Ambrose's teaching. It would be better perhaps to look at various of his writings, where, unpressured by political considerations and public tumult, he voiced in careful words his belief on the matter:

> Therefore the three witnesses in Baptism are one: the water, the blood, and the Spirit; for if you take away one of these, the Sacrament of Baptism does not exist. For what is water without the cross of Christ? A common element without any sacramental effect. Nor does the mystery of regeneration exist at all without water: "For except a man be born again of water and the Spirit, he cannot enter into the Kingdom" (St. John 3:5). Now, even the catechumen believes in the cross of the Lord Jesus, wherewith he also signs himself; but unless he be baptized in the name of the Father, and of the Son, and of the Holy Ghost, he cannot receive remission of his sins nor the gift of spiritual grace. (*De Mysteriis*, Ch. IV., no. 4).

Strangely enough, this quotation is still found in the post-Vatican II Liturgy of the Hours. But St. Ambrose has more to say:

> ...For no one ascends into the Kingdom of Heaven except through the Sacrament of Baptism. No one is excused from Baptism: not infants nor anyone hindered by any necessity. (*De Abraham*, ch. XI, no. 79).

> One is the baptism which the Church administers, the baptism of water and the Holy Ghost, with which catechumens need to be baptized. (*Exposition of Psalm 118*, s. 3)

So we see that St. Ambrose did not in fact teach what is called baptism of desire. What then, did he mean by his speech over Valentinian? Fr. Migne supplies the answer himself (*Patrologia Latina XVI* 412, n. 19). St. Ambrose in fact knew, that Valentinian had indeed been baptized, but was not at liberty to reveal the circumstances of the event, which presumably were bound up with the Emperor's mysterious death. Seen in this light, the three sentences represent no departure from Ambrose's teaching elsewhere; moreover, they are in full keeping with the entire tenor of his speech: vague but reassuring. What was the "grace he desired?" Baptism of course! St. Ambrose is assuring his listeners that Valentinian had indeed been baptized, and so they need not fear for him on that count.

Many theologians (cf. Fr. Karl Rahner) since then have taken these words in their historically incorrect sense. St. Augustine in particular appears at one point to have misread his old mentor's views (although he makes no reference to this passage). In *The City of God* (XIII, 7), he opines:

> I have mind in those unbaptized persons who die confessing the name of Christ. They receive the forgiveness of their sins as completely as if they had been cleansed by the waters of baptism. For He who said: "Unless a man be born again of water and the Holy Ghost, he cannot enter into the kingdom of God" made exceptions in other decisions which are no less universal.

Generally, those who would make St. Augustine out to be a defender of baptism of desire will add two other texts from his writings:

> When we speak of within and without in relation to the Church, it is the position of the heart that we must consider, not that of the body... All who are within in heart are saved in the unity of the ark. (*Treatise on Baptism*, bk. V, 28, no. 39).

> Divine Providence is concerned with men individually as well as with men taken collectively; what God does for each man in particular He Himself knows and they in whom He does it, what

he does for mankind is manifested in history and in prophecy. (*Treatise on the True Religion*, 25, no. 46).

All of which is taken by many in later times to mean that St. Augustine believed strongly that the unbaptized could be saved. Yet he also wrote:

> The fault of our nature remains so deeply impressed in our offspring as to make them guilty even when the guilt of the self-same fault has been washed away in the parents by the remission of sin. The guilt, therefore, of that corruption will remain in the carnal offspring of the regenerated until it also is washed away in them by the laver of regeneration. A regenerated man does not regenerate, but generates sons according to the flesh. So his first birth holds a man in that bondage from which nothing but his second birth delivers him. (Jurgens, Fr. William, *The Faith of the Early Fathers*, III: 1536).

> God does not forgive sins except to those who are baptized. (*To Catechumens on the Creed*, sermon VII: 15)

> No doubt, without Baptism no one can come to God. But not everyone who receives Baptism comes to God. (Migne, *Patrologia Latina*, XXXVIII, p. 559).

> The Lord has determined that the kingdom of Heaven should be conferred only on baptized persons. If eternal life can accrue only to those who have been baptized, it follows, of course, that they who die unbaptized incur everlasting death. (Jurgens, *op. cit.*, 1882).

> No one can find salvation except in the Catholic Church. Outside the Church you can find everything except salvation. You can have dignities, you can have Sacraments, you can sing "Alleluia", answer "Amen," have the Gospels, have faith in the name of the Father, the Son, and the Holy Ghost, and preach it too; but never can you find salvation except in the Catholic Church. (*Sermon to People of Caesarea*, Rouet de Journal, *Enchiridion Patristicum*, no. 1858).

One could go on and on with Augustinian quotes to the same purpose. But the tenor of the vast majority of St. Augustine's writings is the same. The three first quoted passages are virtually the only ones in his voluminous writings which can even appear to support the construction later writers inevitably attempt to foist upon them. But (bearing in mind St. Augustine's Ultra-Realism) it is obvious that in the third passage cited, he is speaking of the manifold ways whereby God draws humans into his Church: some by hearing the Faith preached; others by miraculous intervention, as with the Ethiopian eunuch; still others by flashes of insight of apparent odd happenstances. Yet all are drawn to the same goal.

The second is part of a treatise against the Donatists, who were a set of heretics who had usurped many dioceses throughout North Africa. In the early Church, all those who were in communion with their bishop were considered to have the same beliefs he did. Thus, the bishop being a Donatist, it would be assumed that all those under him would be so equally. But, even though a man might receive the sacraments from the priests of a Donatist bishop, St. Augustine did not believe that such a one was necessarily a sharer in that heresy. The Donatists were a nasty breed, and prone to torturing their opponents; so it would be little surprise if few of those who maintained Catholicism "in their hearts" proclaimed themselves openly. This is a particularly comforting teaching for those of us who may not share our own bishop's Modernism.

It must be admitted that the first quote is a flat contradiction of all else he wrote on the subject. But that very fact ought to give pause to those who would make it St. Augustine's definitive statement on the matter. It would appear that here he was merely echoing (as he thought) St. Ambrose. Yet he does explicitly reject his own statement in the matter in his *On the Gospel of John*, tract 120):

> Such may be the grace of God occasionally towards men, and such their great charity and contrition, that they may have remission, justification, and sanctification before the external Sacraments be received. But here we also learn one necessary lesson: that such persons, nevertheless must of necessity receive the Sacraments appointed by Christ, which whosoever contemns can never be justified.

It is rather intriguing, however, that so many writers on these topics would ignore most of these two saints' writings, in favor of a mere oration in the one case, and an atypical passage bolstered with two irrelevant ones in the others.

The consensus of the Fathers on the necessity of the Church and water baptism for salvation is actually overwhelming. As noted patristic scholar Fr. William Jurgens puts it:

> If there were not a constant tradition in the Fathers that the Gospel message of "unless a man be born again of water, etc.," is to be taken absolutely, it would be easy to say that Our Saviour simply did not see fit to mention the obvious [*to whom?*] exceptions of invincible ignorance and physical impossibility. But the tradition is in fact there, and it is likely enough to be found so constant as to constitute revelation. (*Faith of the Early Fathers,* II, p. 14, n. 31)

Needless to say, the good Father goes on to hedge his statement with all sorts of distinctions; yet he is honest enough to admit the simple teaching of the Fathers.

Nor are the Popes and Councils of the first millennium far behind. Pope St. Zosimus (417-418) approved the following statement:

> On account of this rule of faith, even infants who in themselves have not been able to commit any sin are truly baptized unto the remission of sins, so that the sin they contracted from generation may be cleansed by regeneration. Likewise, if anyone says that it might be understood that, in the kingdom of Heaven, there will be some middle place or some place anywhere that infants live who departed this life without Baptism, without which they cannot enter the kingdom of Heaven which is eternal life: let him be anathema.
>
> For when the Lord says: "Unless one be born again of water and the Holy Ghost, he shall not enter into the kingdom of God" (St. John 3:5), what Catholic will doubt that he will be a partner of the devil who has not deserved to be a co-heir of Christ? (Denzinger 102).

Pope St. Leo I (440-461) wrote in like fashion (Epistle XV: 10; Migne, *Patrologia Latina*, LIV, 581): "Since by transgression of the first man the whole progeny of the human race is vitiated, no one can be freed from the condition of the old man except by the Sacrament of the Baptism of Christ."

ULTRA-REALISM AND THE MIDDLE AGES

So we see that the definitive teaching of the early Church on this topic was quite clear, and at once purely scriptural and completely Ultra-Realist. It would be many centuries before any would seriously question this view of the salvific mission of the Church and Sacraments. Pope St. Pelagius II (578-590) quoted extensively from Ss. Cyprian and Augustine in laying down the necessity of belonging to the Church. Constantinople IV declared that "The first condition for salvation is to keep the rule of the true faith" (Denz. 1833). As Archbishop of Rheims, Pope Sylvester II (Gerbert) penned a "Profession of Faith" dated June, 991. On our topic he writes therein "I believe that in Baptism all sins are forgiven, that one which was committed originally as much as those which are voluntarily committed, and I profess that outside the Catholic Church no one is saved" (*Letters of Gerbert*, Harriet Pratt Lattin, trans.; Columbia University press, New York 1961; p. 224). Coming from one who was not merely a Pope and extremely important Ultra-Realist philosopher, but also a renowned scientist, mathematician (he introduced Arabic numerals to the West), educator, and diplomat, it is testimony which cannot be ignored. It would be tiresome to quote much more, because the vast consensus of magisterial and traditional documents in the early Middle Ages is in favor of the simple view of Salvation first enunciated by Christ.

There is, however, one major exception; an exception so glaring that it has been seized upon by recent and subsequent theologians as a means of giving their teachings in this area the savour of antiquity: we speak of the letter *Apostolicam Sedem*, written at the behest of Pope Innocent II (1130-1143), at an unknown date to an unnamed bishop of Cremona. The latter had written an enquiry to the Pope regarding the case of a priest who apparently had died without being baptized. Of course, it has been defined that, in such a case, he was no priest, since the Sacrament of Orders may only be conferred validly upon the baptized. At any rate, here is the text of the letter:

> To your enquiry we respond thus: We assert without hesitation (on the authority of the Holy Fathers Augustine and Ambrose) that the priest whom you indicated (in your letter) had died without the water of baptism, because he persevered in the faith of Holy Mother the Church and in the confession of the name of Christ, was freed from original sin and attained the key of the heavenly fatherland. Read (brother) in the eighth book of Augustine's "City of God" where among other things it is written, "Baptism is ministered invisibly to one whom not contempt of religion but death excludes." Read again the book of the blessed Ambrose concerning the death of Valentinian where he says the same thing. Therefore, to questions concerning the dead, you should hold the opinions of the learned Fathers, and in your church you should join in prayers and you should have sacrifices offered to God for the priest mentioned. (Denzinger 388).

Now, there are more than a few problems connected with this letter. Firstly, it depends on the witness of Ss. Ambrose and Augustine for its conclusion. Its premises (as we have just seen) are false, as the Fathers in question did not actually hold the opinions herein imputed to them. Secondly, this letter is a private communication regarding a prudential and disciplinary judgment. There is no question of the lack of infallibility of such a document, particularly since it is in direct contradiction to the whole spirit and tenor of Papal acts of the time. Lastly, there is even question of who wrote this letter. Many authorities ascribe it to Innocent III (1198-1216). This question is mentioned in Denzinger. The letter is certainly not in keeping with the totality of his declarations either. In any case, a gap of 55 years separated the two pontificates. So a private letter of uncertain date, authorship, and destination, based upon false premises and contradicting innumerable indisputably valid and solemn documents, is pretended to carry the weight of the Magisterium on its shoulders. Were any other doctrine concerned, this missive would not even be given any consideration. As we shall see, however, mystification and deception are part and parcel of the history of this topic of Salvation. Perhaps the letter was attributed to Innocent III because of his statement that the words of consecration at Mass do not actually have to be said by the priest, but only thought internally—a sort of Eucharist by Desire. Later St. Thomas Aquinas took him to task on this point.

But Innocent III is indeed key to understanding the original teaching of the Church on this topic. It was in his time (as always until the Second Plenary Council of Baltimore) forbidden to bury the unbaptized (whether catechumens or even children of Catholic parents) in consecrated ground. He explained the rationale for this law, writing: "It has been decreed by the sacred canons that we are to have no communion with those who are dead, if we have not communicated with them while alive" (Decr., III, XXVIII, xii). Commenting on this passage for the *Catholic Encyclopedia* (II, 267), William Fanning, a believer in "baptism of desire," nevertheless remarks: "As baptism is the door of the Church, the unbaptized are entirely without its pale."

Innocent III (patron of Ss. Dominic and Francis), was at great pains, however, to distinguish between the eternal fate of unbaptized infants and adults. "The penalty of original sin is the loss of the vision of God; the penalty of actual sin is the torment of everlasting hell" (Denzinger 410). Lack of baptism leaves the individual merely a fallen man, incapable of ascending to Heaven and the beatific vision; actual and unforgiven sin is punished according to its kind. So the Just in the Old Law were confined in the Limbo of their Fathers until Christ freed them: without punishment, because their sins had been forgiven, but without viewing God, because of their very nature. The same was therefore held of unbaptized infants who had no actual sin because of their extreme youth, but were incapable of Heaven because of their humanity. So they too were said to be in a sort of Limbo— "of the Infants." The rest of unbaptized adulthood obviously had greater or lesser sins on their souls, in addition to being part of Fallen Man.

In 1208, Innocent III wrote a profession of Faith to be recited by a group of Waldensian heretics who were being reconciled. Among the other truths, the Pontiff required them to swear that: "By the heart we believe and by the mouth we confess the one Church, not of heretics but the Holy Roman, Catholic, and Apostolic Church outside which we believe no one is saved." (Denzinger 423).

This teaching Innocent III had even more solemnly enunciated by Lateran IV:

> One indeed is the universal Church of the faithful, outside which no one at all is saved, in which the priest himself is the sacrifice, Jesus Christ, whose body and blood are truly contained in the sacrament of the altar under the species of bread and wine; the bread changed into His body by the divine power of transubstantiation, and the wine into the blood, so that to accomplish the mystery of unity we ourselves receive from His nature what He Himself received from ours. (Denzinger 738).

So we see that, for Innocent III, baptism was the entrance into the Church and its attendant other sacraments which were the whole means of salvation. It is true that Denzinger also carries another private letter of this Pontiff, regarding a Jew who attempted, while on the point of death, to baptize himself. Here he says, after declaring that it would not be a real baptism: "If, however, such a one had died immediately, he would have rushed to his heavenly home without delay because of the faith of the sacrament, although not because of the sacrament of faith" (Denzinger 413). This, however, is obviously not an authoritative statement, but Innocent's opinion as a private theologian in a private letter, regarding an admittedly bizarre case. As we see, it contradicts his public and binding pronouncements. Its inclusion in Denzinger is rather more interesting than the letter itself.

What was the opinion of average Catholics during the Middle Ages, the *sensus fidei*, in a time when the Faith permeated every inch of popular culture? Let us look at a few examples.

St. Louis IX, King of France (1214-1270), was in his beliefs typical of educated lay Catholic opinion of his time (and contrary to popular belief, such did indeed exist). His friend, Jehan de Joinville, wrote a biography of him which breathes the spirit of chivalric Christendom. In the 1955 edition of *The Life of St. Louis*, (Rene Hague, trans.) we may see the beliefs of the King quite clearly. The first appendix therein is the *Credo* written at the behest of St. Louis. Explaining the work, de Joinville comments:

> Brother Henry the Teuton, who was a most learned clerk, said that no man could be saved if he did not know his *Credo*; and in order that men might be led to believe what was indispensable to their salvation, I first had this work done at Acre... (p. 224).

Commenting further on about what is required for salvation, de Joinville says:

> Thus we are obliged, so long as we are in this mortal life, to hold God tightly to us with both arms, so that the enemy may not come between us and Him. The two arms with which we must hold God clasped, are firm faith and good works. We need both of these together if we wish to keep hold of God, for either one of them is useless without the other. This you may see in the devils; they firmly believe all the articles of our faith, and yet it is of no use to them, for they do no good works and we can see the contrary in the Saracens and the Albigensian heretics; they do many great penances, but it is of no use to them, for it is written that those who do not believe shall be damned. (p. 236)

This was in truth the belief of our ancestors.

In *The Tale of Sir Hugh of Tabarie*, Sir Hugh is asked by his captor, Saladin, to knight him in return for release. Sir Hugh refuses:

> "Sir, God forbid that I should be so false as to confer so high a gift, even upon the body of so mighty a prince as you... For reason, sire, that your body is but an empty vessel."
> "Empty of what, Sir Hugh?"
> "Sire, of Christianity and of baptism."

So devoted to Baptism were the Medievals that "In our Western provinces, the parents themselves refused to embrace their children before they had been christened" (Gautier, Leon, *Chivalry*, p. 89).

In *The Song of Roland* (c. 1099), after the Moorish Queen, Bramimond, agrees to convert, Charlemagne says:

> Sermon and story on her heart have prevailed
> God to believe and Christendom to take;
> Therefore baptize her that her soul may be saved.

Wolfram von Eschenbach, in *Parzifal*, at the baptism of the hero's Saracen half-brother, Feirefiz, has the priest charge the catechumen:

> You shall believe—and thereby rob the Devil of your soul—
> in the Highest God alone, whose Trinity is universal and everywhere of equal yield. God is man and His Father's Word. As

He is both Father and Son, Who are held in equal honor, and of equal rank with His Spirit, may this water fend heathenry from you with the full power of all Three. By the power of the Trinity He also went into the water for baptism from Whom Adam received his features. From water trees derive their sap. Water fructifies all created things, which man calls creatures. From water man has his sight. Water gives many souls such radiance that angels cannot be more bright.

When Perceval encounters a priest-like figure aboard a miraculous ship in the old French Romance *The Quest of the Holy Grail*, he is told:

> ...before you were baptized into the Christian faith you were in the enemy's [Satan's] thrall. But in the moment you received the seal of Jesus Christ, which is the holy oil with which you were anointed, you renounced the enemy and escaped his jurisdiction, having done homage to the Lord who made you.

The great Dante is not silent either. Taking an even more rigorous stand than some of the Church Fathers, he will not even admit the pagan philosophers, but makes Virgil to say in Canto IV of the *Divine Comedy*:

> Thou asketh not what spirits are these thou seest? I wish thee to know, before thou goest farther, that they sinned not; and though they have merit, it suffices not: for they had not Baptism, which is the portal of the faith that thou believest...

THE CHANGE OCCURS

But a change became apparent in the 14th Century. Venerable Walter Hilton (1340-1396) an Augustinian Canon in England, wrote a book called *The Stairway (or Ladder or Scale) of Perfection*. Therein he addressed a growing theological opinion:

> ...it seems to me that a great and serious error is being made by those men who say that Jews and Saracens can be saved by keeping their own law, even if they don't believe in Jesus Christ as Holy Church believes, inasmuch as they imagine that their own belief is good, secure, and sufficient for their salvation and, in that belief, do (as it seems) many good deeds of justice. And (these

men say) if perchance these Jews and Saracens knew that the Christian faith were better than theirs, they would leave their own faith and accept Christianity. For these reasons, they conclude that these Jews and Saracens can be saved.

No! This is not enough! For Christ, God and man, is both the road and the journey's end. He is the mediator between God and man, and without Him, no soul can be reconciled, nor come to the bliss of Heaven. Therefore, those who do not believe that He is both God and man can never be saved nor come to bliss. (Del Mastro, M.L., trans., p. 196).

Whence came the odd ideas Hilton denounced? From a fairly new school of Philosophy which claimed as its founder one of the greatest minds to ever grace Christendom.

As we have seen, the dominant school of philosophy was what is called Ultra-Realism, or, if one prefers, Christian Neoplatonism. The Church Fathers were of this philosophy, and the Creeds and Liturgies were formed under its influence. Its approach to the question of Salvation was based upon that of the Scriptures, explained using the Platonic view of the Universals. Typical of them were the views of Odo of Tournai (d. 1113), a teacher of the Cathedral school whence comes his name. His view of original sin is encapsulated by Paul Glen (*History of Philosophy,* p. 199) thusly:

> The human race is of one specific substance. At first, this substance was found in only two persons. They sinned, and being the whole human substance, this entire substance was vitiated by their sin. Hence Original Sin is transmitted by natural necessity to all human individuals. New births are not productions of new substances, but are merely new properties of the already existing human substance. Individual men differ only accidentally.

This teaching is rather interesting in the light of the 1311 Council of Vienne, which defined that the soul is the form of the body ("[anyone who]... holds that the rational or intellective soul is not the form of the human body in itself and essentially must be regarded as a heretic." Denz. 481) Considering genetics, which at once determines via an intricate code that, physically, every human being is part of one humanity, and yet is an individual, one cannot help but wonder if the physical pattern is not merely some shadow of the spiritual. God makes each soul anew; but he does it always according to a certain pattern.

At any rate, seeing that the fate of natural man was in fact separation from God, it was easy for the Ultra-Realist to understand that "Outside the Church there is no Salvation"; nothing, given the nature of Baptism and the other sacraments, could make more sense. As the non-Catholic Alfred Weber put it in his *History of Philosophy* (Frank Thilly, trans., pp. 171-172):

> The Catholic or *universal* Church does not merely aim to be an aggregation of particular Christian communities and of the believers composing them; she regards herself as a superior power, as a reality distinct from and independent of the individuals belonging to the fold. If the *Idea*, that is, the general or universal, were not a *reality*, "the Church" would be a mere collective term, and the particular churches, or rather the individuals composing them, would be the only *realities*. Hence, the Church must be [Ultra-] realistic, and declare with the Academy [Plato's School]: Universals are real. Catholicism is synonymous with [Ultra-] realism.

Obviously, if the Church is no more than the sum of her members, she can have no claim to authority over them, no right to call herself "the Mystical Body of Christ," and above all, no right to claim to be the sole means of Salvation. In a word, she must dissolve into her membership, who in turn are thrown upon their own resources for Salvation.

Since Ultra-Realists held that the Will forms the Intellect, reaching men of Good Will was of primary importance. Contrary to popular belief, even in the Middle Ages, when Christendom was at its height, the missionary effort was intense. It is good to remember in this connection that many of the great Spanish and Portuguese Missionaries in both the East and West Indies, as well as the rest of the New World, were Ultra-Realist, exercising what one clerical author puts rather snidely as "the fundamentalistic understanding of the membership requirement, leading to heroic missionary zeal on the part of not a few Saints, anxious to rescue pagans from otherwise certain eternal ruin." *Pace,* the good father, if such an understanding did indeed lead to "heroic missionary zeal" and made Saints (which after all is the only reason for the Church to exist), perhaps those Saints were right and he mistaken?

But it should also be pointed out that Ultra-Realists also believed that, were it necessary, God would bring the Faith to Good-

Willed men miraculously, as he did with the Ethiopian eunuch. So for such, the question of the "ignorant native on the desert island" simply could not arise; if said native was of Good Will he would receive the Faith; if not, an army of Missionaries could not help him—any more than all the priests of Europe could help the bad-willed there.

To understand Ultra-Realism's importance, we would do well to recall a few of its proponents. Apart from St. Dionysius the Areopagite, St. Augustine, and the other Church Fathers, we can mention Alcuin (735-804) founder of Charlemagne's palace school and reviver of learning in the West; John Scotus Eriugena (810-878), the first post-Roman Western philosopher to attempt the synthesis of religion and science, often (falsely) accused of Pantheism; and Gerbert, Pope as Sylvester II (945-1003), whom we have already met, considered a "universal genius." These were the forerunners of scholasticism; Ultra-Realism produced many other great figures subsequently. St. Anselm (1033-1109), archbishop of Canterbury, formulated what may be considered the rallying cry of Ultra-Realism in particular and Christian Philosophy in general: "I believe that I may understand." There were the many brilliant products of the School of Chartres which reached its height in the 12th Century and was a center of Ultra-Realism, functioning with the protection of John of Salisbury (1115-1180). To these should be added Alan of Lille (1128-1202), the "Universal Doctor"; St. Bernard of Clairvaux (1091-1153); and the School of St. Victor, whose famous sons (all bearing the title "of St. Victor"); Hugh, Richard, Walter, and Adam, all distinguished themselves in the not unrelated fields of Ultra-Realist philosophy, Mystical Theology, and Liturgical composition.

The 13th is often called "the greatest of centuries." The schools indeed produced many great Ultra-Realist philosophers in that time—William of Auvergne (d. 1249), called "the first great scholastic;" Alexander of Hales (d. 1249), the "irrefragable doctor", teacher of the great St. Bonaventure; Roger Bacon (1214-1292), inventor of gunpowder who nevertheless taught that Revelation is as important a means of finding truth as experimentation (or more so); Henry of Ghent (d. 1293), the "solemn doctor", and Bl. Raymond Lully, whose clear realization of the interconnectedness of all truth drove him from the University to the Missions—just as it did St. Junipero Serra, his most noted disciple.

What sort of mindset did centuries of Ultra-Realism produce? What was its effect upon the social order? Non-Christian historian Norman F. Cantor gives a good summary:

> In assessing their own world, medieval intellectuals were heavily conditioned by a persistent idealism that saw in society around them signs of the earthly incarnation of the Heavenly City...
> The central dogma of the Incarnation likewise governed the social perceptions of medieval people. They were pre-conditioned by the dogma of the Incarnation, and the philosophy of "realism" that underlies it, to find the ideal within the material, the beautiful within the ugly, the moral and peaceful in the midst of violence and disorder. "The Word was made flesh, and dwelt among us... full of grace and truth." Since everything was of divine creation, medieval intellectuals had no doubt that all the pieces would ultimately fit together in an idealistic, morally committed structure. Whatever they saw or experienced was part of a divine manifestation. (*Inventing the Middle Ages*, p. 414.)

But the 13th Century, the very flowering of the Medieval synthesis, saw the beginning of the end of this thoroughly consistent worldview, replete as it was with practical mysticism, and mystical pragmatism. The reason was the rediscovery through Arab sources of Aristotle, as a result of the Crusades. There were several reasons why Aristotelianism would act as a solvent upon the Medieval worldview. We shall examine several of them, but the first and worst is that of the "Double Truth," that what is true in religion can be false in philosophy (taken as learning in its widest sense). Strictly speaking, this was created by the Arab Aristotelian, Averroes; but it came West with the works of the Master.

THE NEW PHILOSOPHY
AND ST. THOMAS

Although Aristotle's works were placed in the curriculum of the University of Paris in 1252, St. Albertus Magnus (1193-1280) was the first great scholastic to experiment with integrating Aristotelianism with the Faith. But the greatest exponent of this work was his illustrious pupil, St. Thomas Aquinas (1225-1274).

Today, when Thomism has long since been considered the Catholic philosophy *par excellence*, it is easy to forget that at its inception it was considered revolutionary. How did it differ from Ultra-Realism? Well, Moderate Realism, as Aristotelianism and its daughter philosophies are called, holds, firstly that outside the mind there are no universal essences; only individual things. But the Universals do have a certain reality, as the traits associated with them can be found in each individual. This may seem like a small point, but it has great effects, for the Moderate Realists hold that the Intellect precedes the Will. The result is that, if an individual has not been trained to want the good, he cannot want the good, generally speaking. He becomes the prisoner of his upbringing. This idea would have catastrophic results later.

The danger in Aristotelianism was recognized at the time, and even some modern authorities have seen it:

> The synthesis perfected by thirteenth-century Scholasticism and most perfectly by its greatest representative, St. Thomas, was a synthesis of human wisdom and Divine revelation; in philosophy, between Augustinian Neoplatonism, with its one-sided emphasis on the vertical and spiritual movement, and the more humanist and scientifically rationalist philosophy of Aristotle. St. Thomas vindicated the autonomy of philosophy, the power of the human mind to attain truth by its natural light and the relative independence of created causes. In some points even, I venture to think, he inclined too far in the rationalist and Aristotelian direction. For example, he regarded the sense as the

sole ultimate source of human knowledge. And by denying spiritual matter and, therefore, making the body the principle of man's individuation, he rendered it very difficult to understand how the individual can survive death. We may prefer in some respects the teaching of the more Platonic Bonaventure. (E.I. Watkins, *Catholic Art and Culture*, pp. 94-95).

Fr. John Coony in his *How Brief a Candle*, goes into a bit more detail:

> Obviously, the world of the thirteenth century was not the same as that of which Aristotle wrote. Many concepts had changed, but while the concepts had changed, the basic principles of reasoning on which they were developed had not. The problem in adaptation was one of updating the concepts while maintaining the basic principles and methodology intact. This was the procedure to which Thomas set himself. He had manifest difficulties. The chief theologic problems with Aristotle were: first, he did not mention a Creator; second, his world was eternal, subject only to deterministic forces; third, he provided a God who, while supplying energy to the system, was wholly indifferent to man's problems; fourth, man was only matter and religious values did not enter into the concept of moral perfection. Finally, as noted above, man was on his own, and individually his intelligence did not continue to exist after his death.
>
> Thomas' opponents were principally those who believed that the only proper source of all philosophy was Plato and his followers, especially St. Augustine. Plato, particularly in the concept of the Creator, the loving model of Goodness, remained in Thomas' *Summa Theologica*, but this was not enough for the strict Platonists.
>
> ...Despite his rousing refutation of Siger [of Brabant, a philosopher who reveled in the Double Truth], Thomas was brought the first time to realize the misconstruction which the others could place on his work. Others, after Siger, could twist the statements to the effect that there were... two completely incompatible truths... Shortly before his death, Thomas Aquinas is reported to have said to his associates, "Everything I have written is as so much straw compared with the realities." He did not complete his *Summa*. (pp. 55-56).

Yet, it may be that all the criticisms against his work were not based upon mere malice. Certainly, he did contribute to the widening between Theology and Philosophy. His rejection of the Immaculate Conception was based upon erroneous Aristotelian "Science" (despite the witness of scripture, Tradition, and the Liturgy); his "principle of contradiction" (something cannot be one and many at once) would appear to make the plurality of the Blessed Sacrament in time and space impossible (a charge which will bring the reply from his defenders that this is a different thing—a miracle, and so outside the bounds of philosophy. Your author would then answer triumphantly with "Aha! The Double Truth!"); he rejected the Ultra-Realist notion of Illumined Knowledge, although he himself apparently possessed it on certain points (most notably the Eucharist); there are indeed many problems here. So many, indeed, that St. Bonaventure, his close friend, called him "the Father of all Heresies!" But these were implicit in the Aristotelian methodology he had adopted. Even the Church herself would become indefinable under Thomistic principles: if "Church" is a Universal, and Universals derive their reality from their concrete manifestations, then the Church could only be a reflection of her membership. She would be faithful to her calling only in so far as she accurately represented their views and actions. Under these circumstances, of course, she could not be Divine.

However, when St. Thomas threw Aristotle to the winds, as he did with his treatment of the Blessed Sacrament, he was sublime. Indeed, Urban IV asked both St. Bonaventure and himself to write alternative offices for the Feast of Corpus Christi. When his Franciscan friend (for so St. Bonaventure was) read St. Thomas' submission, he burned his own. And of course, where Aristotle can be useful, in some of the more mundane things, like government, St. Thomas also shines. The obvious fact of his sanctity is of course important in evaluating him, though by itself it does not canonize his philosophy. Saints are canonized for heroic virtue, not for philosophical ability.

St. Dominic and St. Francis had been good friends; so too were St. Bonaventure, OFM. And St. Thomas Aquinas, OP. Indeed, one wishes all Franciscans and Dominicans had gotten on so well as did their founders and two leading lights throughout subsequent history. But St. Bonaventure was an Ultra-Realist, and St. Thomas Aquinas a Moderate Realist. Fr. Coony contrasts their two positions well:

> The old Platonic-Augustinian or traditional concept saw the apex of man's dignity in that of sanctity achievable through mystical union with God in a life of intense contemplation. Man's individual dignity depended upon his own freely-willed response to God. Authority and revelation were the primary guides; reason was supporting. Man's dignity rests in his relationship to God. This was a continuation of the old monastic ideal...
>
> A second path was that of Thomas' main line scholastics, who agreed fundamentally with the first, but placed greater emphasis on the ability of man to achieve true knowledge and on the value of intellectual, rather than emotive or intuitive, motivation in approach to God. They gave about equal weight to reason, authority, and revelation as sources of knowledge of God—though in case of conflict revelation and authority would control. This group logically includes those who followed William of Ockham, the Nominalists [who taught that the Universals were mere names]. (Coony, *op. cit.,* p. 69)

The same theme is developed from the point of view of an admirer of St. Bonaventure, Effrem Bettoni:

> The Platonist sees things in God; the Aristotelian sees God at the summit of things. If both philosophies lead to religion, it is undeniable that the religious element is more spontaneous in a philosophy of the Platonic type for it penetrates its very structure. (*St. Bonaventure*, Angelus Gambatese, OFM., trans., p. 20).

Ultra-Realists were known in the Middle Ages as "Ancients," while their opponents were called "Moderns." Hence opposition to St. Thomas came from very many traditionally-minded sources, quite apart from his friend St. Bonaventure. In his own Dominican Order, he was opposed by Roland of Cremona, Robert Fitzacre, Hugh of St. Cher, and Peter of Tarentaise. The Franciscans William De La Mare, Richard of Middleton, Matthew of Aquasparta, William of Falgar, Peter Olivi, Roger Marston, and Bl. Duns Scotus likewise rejected Thomism, as did the secular clerics Henry of Ghent, William of St. Amour, and Gerard of Abbeville. In 1277, four years after his death, the University of Paris condemned Thomism, which condemnation was repeated by Oxford University a few days later at the request of the Dominican Archbishop of Canterbury, Robert Kilwardby. His successor, John Peckham, renewed the condemnation in 1284 and 1286. These were lifted at last after Aquinas' canonization in 1324. Thomism in more or less dilute form was adopted by the Dominican Order thereafter as its official teaching, and Thomist influence spread throughout the Church, helping for example, to delay the definition of the Immaculate Conception until 1854. For many centuries, adherence to this dogma was tantamount to anti-Thomism.

All of this is necessary background for considering St. Thomas' opinion on baptism and membership in the Church as requirements for Salvation; there can be no doubt that most adherents of "desire" look to the *Summa* and St. Thomas for justification of their stand. So, in the *Summa* (Part III, qu. 68, art. 3) we read:

> ...the sacrament of Baptism may be wanting to anyone in reality but not in desire: for instance, when a man wishes to be baptized, but by some ill-chance he is forestalled by death before receiving Baptism. And such a man can obtain salvation without being actually baptized, on account of his desire for Baptism, which desire is the outcome of *faith that worketh by charity*, whereby God, whose power is not tied to visible sacraments, sanctifies man inwardly. Hence Ambrose says of Valentinian, who died while yet a catechumen: *I lost him whom I was to regenerate: but he did not lose the grace he prayed for.*

Aquinas has spoken; surely the case is closed? No. Firstly, as we have seen, those words of Ambrose do not carry the meaning the Angelic Doctor believe them to hold; one can only wish he had studied Ambrose as carefully as he did Aristotle at the times these lines were written. Further, his line about God's power not being tied to His visible Sacraments is very questionable. For God, who could transubstantiate Himself into anything will only do it into Bread and Wine. He only grants Orders through Chrism, Marriage through vowing and consummation, and so on. Anything is possible to Him, but He binds Himself into certain patterns; we may only be concerned with those He communicates in Revelation—and that, as we have seen, is very definite about Baptism. Its graces work through water, just as all the other sacraments work through other physical things. But it is difficult for an Aristotelian to see this. Similarly, the whole concept of a catechumen being killed "by some ill-chance," surely leaves out entirely the providence of God and thrusts us into Aristotelian determinism. God was apparently out shopping when the ill-chance struck.

In any case, St. Thomas is not really a good witness for Baptism of Desire, any more than St. Augustine or St. Ambrose. In his *Catena Aurea*, he writes: "It is not enough merely to believe. He who believes and is not yet baptized, but is only catechumen, has not yet fully acquired salvation." Even in the *Summa* itself, he contradicts himself (part III, Qu. 65, art. 4): "A thing may be so necessary that, without it, the end cannot be attained... In this way the Sacrament of Baptism is necessary to the individual, simply and absolutely." There is no sacrament without the matter—water. Further, as we know, without actual water Baptism a man cannot be made subject to the Pope, and according to St. Thomas' *Against the Errors of the Greeks*, Pt. II, Ch. 36: "To be subject to the Roman Pontiff is absolutely necessary for Salvation." All of this is contrary to what Modern Thomists (whether of the "Neo" or "Transcendental" varieties) would hold. But, judging by his rejection of the only one of his works such folk generally consult, St. Thomas does not appear to have really been a Thomist in the Modern sense of the term, however much their various schools may employ ideas implicit in his work.

Nevertheless, the rise of Aristotelianism in general presaged some radical disruption in the order of things. The old Ultra-Realist view, applied to the social order, is well summed up by James, Viscount Bryce, in his *The Holy Roman Empire* (pp. 102-105):

> The realistic philosophy, and the needs of a time when the only notion of civil or religious order was submission to authority, required the World State to be a monarchy: tradition, as well as the continued existence of a part of the ancient institutions, gave the monarch the name of Roman Emperor. A king could not be universal sovereign, for there were many kings: the Emperor must be universal, for there had never been but one Emperor; he had in older and brighter days been the actual lord of the civilized world; the seat of his power was placed beside that of the spiritual autocrat of Christendom. His functions will be seen most clearly if we deduce them from the leading principle of medieval mythology [as the ignorant call it], the exact correspondence of earth and heaven. As God, in the midst of the celestial hierarchy, rules blessed spirits in Paradise, so the Pope, His vicar, raised above priests, bishops, metropolitans, reigns over the souls of mortal men below. But as God is Lord of earth as well as of heaven, so much he (the *Imperator coelestis*) be represented by a second earthly viceroy, the Emperor (*Imperator terrenus*), whose

authority shall be of and for this present life. And as in this present world the soul cannot act save through the body, while yet the body is no more than an instrument and means for the soul's manifestation, so there must be a rule and care of men's bodies as well as of their souls, yet subordinated always to the well-being of that element which is the purer and more enduring. It is under the emblem of soul and body that the relation of the papal and imperial power is presented to us throughout the Middle Ages. The Pope, as God's vicar in matters spiritual, is to lead men to eternal life; the Emperor, as vicar in matters temporal, must so control them in their dealings with one another that they are able to pursue undisturbed the spiritual life, and thereby attain the same supreme and common end of everlasting happiness. In view of this object his chief duty is to maintain peace in the world, while towards the Church his position is that of Advocate or Patron, a title borrowed from the practice adopted by churches and monasteries of choosing some powerful baron to protect their lands and lead their tenants in war. The functions of Advocacy are twofold: at home to make the Christian people obedient to the priesthood, and to execute priestly decrees upon heretics and sinners; abroad to propagate the faith among the heathen, not sparing to use carnal weapons. Thus does the Emperor answer in every point to his antitype the Pope, his power being yet of a lower rank, created on the analogy of the papal... Thus the Holy Roman Church and the Holy Roman Empire are one and the same thing, seen from different sides; and Catholicism, the principle of the universal Christian society, is also Romanism.

Inspired by their pet scholars, the various Kings imagining themselves in proper Aristotelian fashion to have power independent from the Divine Order, began to build the beginnings of the modern State, and to reject the supra-national authority of Church and Empire. It was in the face of increasing usurpations of Ecclesiastical rights by Philip the Fair of France that Boniface VIII issued the Bull *Unam Sanctam*. The first part of the Bull laid down the relations of the Papacy to the Temporal power. It was not, however, characterized by the doctrinal and *ex cathedra* (and thus infallible) nature of the last part, which we now reproduce:

> Urged by faith, We are obliged to believe and to hold that the Church is one, holy, catholic, and also apostolic. We firmly believe in Her, and We confess absolutely that outside of Her there is neither salvation nor the remission of sins... Furthermore,

We declare, say, define, and pronounce that it is wholly necessary for the salvation of every human creature to be subject to the Roman Pontiff. (Denzinger 468).

In light of what has just been said, it will surprise no one that Boniface VIII was assisted by an Ultra-Realist (though not unfriendly to Thomism) philosopher, the Augustinian Giles of Rome in composing this Bull.

Of course, Boniface VIII was attacked by the French, and the 14th Century was scandalized by the Babylonian Captivity and the Great Schism, all of which dragged the Papacy's reputation down into the dust. Then followed the Conciliarist controversy. Ironically, however, at the Council of Florence both Baptism and the necessity of the Church for Salvation were clearly defined. In the Bull *Exultate Deo*, 22 November 1439, issued at the behest of the Armenians who were reentering union with Rome, Baptism is thusly described:

> Holy Baptism, which is the gateway to spiritual life, holds the first place among the sacraments; through it we are made members of Christ and of the Body of the Church. And since death entered into the universe through the first man, "unless we are born of water and Spirit, we cannot" as the Truth says, "enter into the kingdom of heaven." The matter of this sacrament is real and natural water; it makes no difference whether cold or warm. (Denzinger 696)

There is no question here of Baptism of Desire, of God not being bound to the Sacraments. Three years later, on 4 February 1441, at the request of similarly reconciling Syrian Jacobites, at the same Council, Eugene IV issued the Bull *Cantate Domino,* which states solemnly:

> The most Holy Roman Church firmly believes, professes and preaches, that none of those existing outside the Catholic Church, not only pagans, but also Jews and heretics and schismatics, can have a share in life eternal; but that they will go into the eternal fire, "which was prepared for the devil and his angels," unless before death they are joined with Her; and that so important the unity of this ecclesiastical body that only those remaining within this unity can profit by the sacraments of the Church unto salvation, and they alone can receive an eternal recompense for

their fasts, their almsgiving, their other works of piety, and the duties of a Christian soldier. No one, let his almsgiving be as great as it may, no one, even if he pour out his blood for the name of Christ, can be saved, unless he remain within the bosom and the unity of the Catholic Church. (Denzinger 715).

There is no hint of ambiguity. Because they were dealing with Ultra-Realist Easterners, the Pope and Council Fathers passed non-Thomist decrees. The last sentence of *Cantate Domino* would appear to eliminate even Baptism of Blood. Yet it is again interesting that Modern theologians will either ignore or explain away both this decree and *Unam Sanctam*. The idea that these words might have been chosen because they were, in fact, intended appears to have escaped them.

It is interesting also to note in this connection that the Union with Constantinople was short. The fall of that City to the Turks in 1452 led to their placing Gennadios II on the Patriarchial throne. A hater of the Latins, he abrogated the Union. But ironically, rather than sharing the Platonism which was and is characteristic of Eastern theology and philosophy, Gennadios was a Thomist. Even more ironic, he differed from St. Thomas in holding the Immaculate Conception, which later Eastern Orthodox theologians have attacked as a Western innovation. Apparently, their theologians do not know their own history.

A NEW THEOLOGY FOR A NEW WORLD

The discovery of America in 1492 led to yet another revolution in theology.

The modern church had adopted the medieval form of baptism as normative, and it had accepted the medieval theology of baptism as definitive. There were no major developments in Catholic baptismal theology after the time of the counter-reformation and only one minor one. The fathers and the scholastics had spoken of "baptism of desire" [not much, as we have seen], by which they meant the desire to be baptized, but after the discovery that the world was larger than Christian Europe some Catholic theologians began to interpret this in a broader sense. It seemed unfair that millions of people were to be condemned to eternal punishment just because they had never heard the message of Christ. Especially when it was learned that non-Christians were not always savage idol-worshippers and that some of their religions prescribed moral standards which matched those of Christianity, it seemed impossible to attribute such a terrible retribution to a merciful God.

So slowly "baptism of desire" came to mean a desire to lead a good and upright life, a desire to live like a Christian so to speak, which was thwarted not by personal fault but by the Church's failure to bring the sacrament to lands it never heard of. (Joseph Martos, *Doors to the Sacred*, pp. 196-197)

This is a rather ignorant view, although it contains some fact. Obviously, Ven. Walter Hilton had refuted the idea of salvation through works by non-Catholics back in the 1300s. Similarly, we have seen Sir Hugh of Tabarie admiring the merely natural virtues of Saladin—but he did not regard them as salvific. Still, the question of the newly discovered Indians (for Medieval Europe knew of China and Africa being non-Christian) did bother academic theologians.

As noted, for the Ultra-Realists, there was no problem. Knowing that God enlightens every man of Good Will, they supposed that the Faith would be given to those who would accept it. For the now-dominant Thomists, though, believing that the Intellect formed the Will, there was indeed a problem. For these, most notably Francisco Suarez, S.J. (1548-1617), the fact of all these intellects forming wills in total absence of Revelation was a threat to the mercy and justice of God; having an Aristotelian view of man, they could not see that the problem was one of Will and Human Nature, rather than of mere individual conduct. At any rate, taking the principle of Invincible Ignorance from Moral Theology (where it was maintained that those raised in ignorance of the sinfulness of, say, theft, would not sin when stealing thereby), they applied it to the question of salvation. Thus, an individual raised without, as they thought, any way of learning the truth, could be saved by his purely human desire for goodness. Needless to say, these were the ruminations of academic theologians. The actual experience of missionaries in the field contradicted them.

In the first place, it must be born in mind that Christianity early took root down the length of the Nile River, in India, Arabia, and Persia. The so-called Nestorians brought the Sacraments throughout the interior of Central Asia and into China, converting the Khan who became known in the West as "Prester John." As we shall see, where the Apostolic Succession remains, heresy tends to degenerate; it were not too outrageous to propose that some simple souls, baptized, communed, believing in the Apostle's Creed, and (as only the simple can be) unconscious of the politics of their *Catholicos* vis-à-vis Rome, may have lived and died as Catholics. For that matter, we have records of the many Latin friars who evangelized Central Asia and China, even founding dioceses. In time, many of these efforts petered out; but the secret history of Asian and African evangelization will make quite a read when at last it is opened on the Day of Judgment.

The history of the Americas is quite as, and even more, interesting from this point of view. In the article "Mexico," in the *Catholic Encyclopedia*, (X, p. 252), there is a fascinating account of pre-Columbian Mexican religion. Some of their ancient traditions closely parallel various stories from Genesis, and represent their particular remnants of the original revelation given the first men. But other elements have a later origin.

In the history of the nations of ancient Mexico the coming of Quezalcoatl marks a distinct era. He was said to have come from the province of Panuco, a white man, of great stature, broad brow, large eyes, long black hair, rounded beard, and dressed in a tunic covered with black and red crosses. Chaste, intelligent, a lover of peace, versed in the arts and sciences, he preached by his example and doctrine a new religion which inculcated fasting and penance, love and reverence for the Divinity, practice of virtue, and hatred of vice. (C.E.X., p. 252).

He went on to predict the coming of white men at a particular time and place (which "just happened" to be the time and place when and where Cortez arrived) who would overthrow their old gods. He was driven out and went to Yucatan with the same message; among the Mayans he was called Kukulcan. From his time in both areas dates the native veneration of the Cross, and in various places there were practiced rites he had introduced, suggestive of our baptism, confession, and communion. The Mayans who practiced the latter called the bread *Toyolliatlacual*: "food of our souls." The author of the article supposes that Quetzalcoatl was a 10th or 11th Century Norse priest, driven off course perhaps from the Northern voyages. Others suggest that he was some disciple of the Irish St. Brendan the Navigator, or even the Saint himself. Whatever the case, the implications of the song written by Cauch, High Priest of Tixcayon, long before the Spanish came are clear:

> There shall come the sign of a god who dwells on high,
> And the cross which illumined the world shall be made manifest;
> The worship of false gods shall cease.
> Your father comes, O Itzalanos!
> Your brother comes, O Itzalanos!
> Receive your bearded guests from the East,
> Who come to bring the sign of God.
> God it is who comes to us, meek and holy.

It is interesting to note that Our Lady appeared at Guadalupe in the traditional garb of an Aztec princess. This 1531 apparition was the signal for mass conversion. Ancient Peru also had a Quetzalcoatl-like figure, Viracocha, who is said to have been an old bearded white man wearing a robe and carrying a staff.

The Vikings, while still pagan, had chased Irish monks from Iceland. Upon their settlement of Greenland, they found evidence that the same group had preceded them, and then fled westward. According to the *Vinland Saga*, the Indians the Norse later encountered on the coast of North America informed them of white bearded men in the interior, who wearing robes carried crosses in procession. The Vikings assumed that these were still more of the same. They themselves maintained a diocese in Greenland from the tenth Century until the 1400s, when the Greenland colony died out. We have, of course, no way of knowing what, if any, missionary activity they undertook, whether collectively or via lone individuals.

Then there is the famous tale of Madoc ap Owain Gwynedd, the legendary Welsh Prince who many claim led a party of colonists to North America in 1170. The legends of "white Indians" bearing tattered Missals, crucifixes, rosaries, etc. appears to have some basis in fact: Roman coins (then in circulation in Wales) have been discovered in Kentucky, where such a group was rumored to exist around Louisville in the 16th Century. Lewis and Clark were very surprised by the Caucasian appearance of many of the Mandan Indians; artist George Catlin who lived among them before their near destruction by small-pox, and knew them better than any other white man, claimed their language contained a great many Welsh words. Whatever the case, the Daughters of the American Revolution felt the story had enough proof to erect the monument to Madoc at the supposed site of his landing in Mobile Bay.

There are many other stories of these kinds; in the absence of written records, however, pre-Columbian America will always be veiled from our eyes by a shroud. Yet it is obvious that there was some contact; it cannot be doubted that these contacts resulted in the bringing of the Faith to the Native Americans of Good Will. Subsequent, more easily verifiable and more miraculous contacts assure us of this.

Most spectacular and best known of these is the experience of Venerable Maria de Agreda (1602-1665). At that time, the first Franciscan missionaries reached the tribes of West Texas and Eastern New Mexico. Much to their surprise, the Padres found that a few of the tribes were already aware of Catholicism, knew its doctrines, and asked for Baptism. When asked how they knew, they replied that they had been taught by a lady in blue. Several of the

Friars returned to Spain, and found Maria de Agreda, head of a convent of nuns who wore blue habits; she claimed to have bilocated to the New World to instruct Indians there for nine years. Questioned in detail about the appearances and customs of those she allegedly had taught, she described to them perfectly the tribes they had just left. The account is commemorated in a mural at the entrance to the Cathedral of Fort Worth, Texas. But why did she go to those tribes, rather than others? Good Will, one must suppose. At any rate, one who was inspired by her example was the Apostle of California, St. Junipero Serra.

A professor of Lullist philosophy, he followed the example of his mentor, and went to California, eventually founding the string of Missions which were the start of its modern culture. Upon his arrival in 1771 at the future site of Mission San Antonio de Padua (near present day Jolon) in central California, he immediately unloaded a bell from a mule, hung it on a tree, and rang it. All the while he shouted "O ye gentiles! Come to the holy church!" His associates reminded him that there were neither Indians nor a church about, to which he replied that he just wanted to "give vent to my desires that this bell might be heard all over the World!" But shortly thereafter, an old Indian woman came into the camp, asking to be baptized. The padres were quite shocked, seeing that there had been no one there to explain the sacrament or its need to the Indians. But the woman explained that her father had told her about a man who appeared to him four times, explaining to him the doctrines of Catholicism. Satisfying their questions, she was forthwith baptized.

Nor are these sorts of things unknown in more recent times. The career of the Belgian Fr. Pierre De Smet (1801-1873), Apostle of the American West, was filled with all sorts of wonders. The Flathead Indians of Montana had heard in the first few years of the 19th Century of Catholicism from Iroquois traders who ventured out to Montana. In the words of John Upton Terrell:

> Profoundly concerned about their own spiritual state, the Flatheads and the Nez Perces gradually turned to the Iroquois for guidance, and they adopted the rites and customs of the Church performed by them. They came to believe what the stern and stoical Iroquois maintained—that the Indian religion was false and that the Flatheads and Nez Perces were in danger of being thrown into hell. Salvation could be achieved only by embracing the Catholic Faith.

They sent several expeditions to St. Louis, hoping to have a "Blackrobe" sent to them. Finally, in 1839, Fr. De Smet answered their call. They converted rapidly. Even the Virgin herself appeared among them: in one instance, a little boy described a Lady in a strange robe standing on a serpent with an apple in its mouth; on another occasion, a twelve-year-old girl lay dying. "How beautiful!" she cried, "how beautiful! I see the heavens opening and the Mother of God is calling me to come." Turning to her survivors, she said, "Heed what the Blackrobes tell you, for they speak the truth." Assisted by these and many other miraculous events, Fr. De Smet eventually baptized 40,000 Indians in 36 different tribes. A Jesuit, he hoped to form a second Paraguay. But the rising power of the United States assured that this did not happen.

Even so, such things go on in our own day as well. *The Religious Memoirs* of Sir Henry Taylor, former Governor-General of the Bahamas (1988-1992), are replete with various marvels in the life of this first Catholic in remote Long Island. Therein he tells the story of a Mrs. Mary Cartwright of Hamiltons, Long Island. On hearing in 1929 that Taylor was bringing a priest to the Island to visit (he himself having converted in 1925), the septuagenarian Mrs. Cartwright asked him for notification when the priest should arrive. When Fr. Dennis Parnell arrived from Nassau, she came to see him, and began to speak:

> "Fr. Dennis," she started, "I am so glad that you have at last arrived. I have been looking for a Catholic priest for a long time, so I must welcome you to Long Island. Fr. Dennis," she continued, "my husband is dead. He died some years ago. He was an invalid and could not get out of bed for thirty-eight years. I attended him during all those years, and we had many private talks together. He was a good man, Father. There were times when he would ask all of us in the bedroom to leave, because he wanted to be alone, and at those times he said that the angels came into his room and ministered to him. There were times when I watched him while he raised his hand to his mouth as if he was receiving Communion."
>
> "Father Dennis and I were both listening intently." She continued, "Father, just before he died, he called me to his bedside and said to me, 'Mary, I am about to leave you, I am about to die. I want to tell you, that before you die, the light of the Catholic Church will come to Long Island. Follow it.'

She paused and looked intently at the priest. There was silence in the room for a few minutes.

"I have been waiting for this day, Father," she said; "I have been looking for you. Now you are here, I am in your hands." Mrs. Cartwright was duly received, and the Church in Long Island dates its origin from this visit.

Less supernatural but no less wondrous means have brought about the foundation of the Church in other lands. In Korea, for example, a Korean nobleman, on an embassy bringing the annual tribute to the Chinese Emperor (the only foreign travel permitted to Koreans at the time) in the mid-18th Century discovered the Chinese writings, explaining Catholicism, of Fr. Matteo Ricci, S.J. at the Imperial Library in Peking. Returning to his own country, he translated them into Korean and circulated them. The result was that when the first Catholic missionary, a Chinese priest, reached Korea in 1795, he was confronted by 4000 neophytes.

None of these occurrences would be strange to the Ultra-Realist philosophers, who would point out that they merely confirmed the fact that God will indeed get the Faith to anyone of Good Will, wherever they may be.

In this context, it will be useful to get the opinion of St. Francis Xavier (1506-1552), who has rightly been called the "greatest Apostle since St. Paul." In his career, he evangelized the peoples of Socotra off the Arabian coast; Goa, Tinnevelli, Travancore, Meliapur, Sao Thome and Cochin in India; Manara and Jaffna in Ceylon; Malacca in Malaysia; Ambon, Ternate, and Moro in Indonesia; numerous places in Japan; ending his life finally on a small island off the coast of China, looking to the new country he wished to evangelize. In the course of his ten years in the East, he baptized 3,000,000 souls.

All of this work was accompanied by much hard labour, disputation, and organization. But it was also assisted by miracles— apparitions, prophecy, discernment of souls, and the like. Most useful of all, given the incredible number of races with which he had to deal, he had the gift of tongues. Speaking to mixed mobs in his own Spanish, they all understood him as though he spoke each of their own languages. It should be apparent, both by his success and by the gifts Heaven showered on his work, that he had the Divine favor. Why did he do it? Because, in common with virtually all Catholics of his time (save some of those locked in the ivory towers of academe), he believed that only the waters of baptism could regenerate their natures and so make Heaven available to them. This we may see by several of his writings. There is, for instance, the prayer he composed, which was recited every year in his honor during the Novena of Grace:

> Eternal God, Creator of all things, remember that the souls of unbelievers have been created by Thee and formed to Thy own image and likeness.
> Behold, O Lord, how to thy dishonor hell is being filled with these very souls.
> Remember that Jesus Christ, Thy Son, for their salvation suffered a most cruel death.
> Do not permit, O Lord, I beseech Thee, that Thy Divine Son be any longer despised by unbelievers, but rather, being appeased by the prayers of thy saints and of the Church, the most holy spouse of Thy Son, deign to be mindful of Thy mercy and forgetting their idolatry and unbelief, bring them to Him Whom Thou didst send, Jesus Christ, Thy Son, Our Lord, Who is our health, life, and resurrection, through Whom we have been redeemed and saved, to Whom be all glory forever. Amen.

In his letters home he repeated over and over again that all who die without the Faith go to Hell—and so he spread that Faith to as many as would take it.

That this was not merely the belief of some crazed miracle worker in the East (although authentic miracles might lead one to question just who is crazy in this regard) is easily proven by looking at the Creed of Pope Pius IV (1559-1565). Incorporating all that previous Creeds had held, together with the definitions of Trent in matters disputed by the Protestants, it includes the words: "This true Catholic faith, outside of which no one can be saved..." (Denzinger 1000). But this brings us to Trent, and yet another Ambrose-Augustine style misunderstanding.

Much is made of a statement made by the Council of Trent (Chap. 4, Session 6) that men cannot obtain justification except by "the laver of regeneration or its desire." But the word used here is *votum,* which is not some nebulous desire to be good, but more an actual vow to do something—it is a strong word. It must further be understood that Justification is not the same thing as Salvation. Justification is being in the State of Grace, free from sin.

Salvation is, ultimately, taking on the Divine Nature, being inserted into Christ forever. Your author, when he steps out from the Confessional, is Justified (assuming he made a good confession). But he is not saved. The difference between him and the catechumen, is that he has been regenerated, and the catechumen not; your author is no longer part of fallen man. Correspondingly, should both he and the catechumen die and go to Hell, your author's torments shall be much greater, precisely because of the baptismal mark upon his soul. It should be remembered, both in your author's case and that of the catechumen, that Justification is a free and unmerited act of Grace on God's part; it is also the commencement of the long journey toward salvation (long in effort, rather than necessarily in time). On that journey we may merit as much as we can; but the grace of final perseverance at the end is also an unmerited Grace—hence our request in the Ave to Our Lady to pray for us at "the hour of our death." So Christ is indeed the Alpha and the Omega, the beginning and the end of the journey. Beyond that, however, your author will say nothing: before him rears up the abyss of Graces versus Free Will, whence many a greater mind than his has foundered. He will not attempt, therefore (knowing his limitations) to pierce that veiled Mystery, but will guide you back to the safer ground of Infallible Pronouncements.

Further proof of this assertion may be seen in other pronouncements of Trent, within the context of which this one must be taken:

> Canon 5. If anyone shall say that baptism is optional, that is, not necessary for salvation, let him be anathema. (Denzinger 861).
>
> Canon 23. If anyone says that a man once justified can avoid all sins, even venial sins, throughout his life without a special privilege of God, as the Church holds in regard to the Blessed Virgin: let him be anathema. (Denzinger 833)
>
> Canon 2. If anyone says that true and natural water is not necessary in Baptism, and therefore interprets metaphorically the words of Our Lord Jesus Christ: Unless one be born again of water and the Holy Ghost...": let him be anathema. (Denzinger 858).
>
> Without our Catholic Faith, it is impossible to please God. (Denzinger 787).

So we see that, taken in context, the oft-quoted text merely says that the vow to receive Baptism may produce in the vow-maker

Justification. This is not the same as Salvation, which can only come about if the individual goes ahead and receives the Sacrament and then finally perseveres. To believe otherwise would indeed make a metaphor of our Lord's words. To be fair, it is alleged by some that this Canon was enacted to prevent an alleged widespread love of baptizing in beer. It is true that Pope Gregory IX (1227-1241) did indeed, in a letter to Sigurd, Archbishop of Nidaros, Norway, dated 8 July 1241, condemn the practice which a lack of water in Scandinavia (?!) had precipitated. (It takes water to make beer!) But it is a bit dishonest to explain away a Canon of Trent with an issue closed and resolved for three centuries. Really, they must try better than that!

The *Catechism of the Council of Trent* can give us further insight into Trent's teaching on the matter. Unfortunately (and perhaps tellingly) most recent English translations have altered the words dealing in this area. But the 1985 Daughters of St. Paul edition, translated by Fr. Robert I. Bradley and Msgr. Eugene Kevane and entitled *The Roman Catechism* suffers from no such distortion—possibly because the vast number of ambiguous Vatican II statements which can be used as footnotes obviate any such need with apparently equally solemn pronouncements. Saving those annotations, though, it is the best and most official catechism in existence. Let us see what it says:

> 31. The Necessity of Baptism
>
> What we have considered thus far regarding Baptism is all very important. Yet what we must consider now is even more so, viz., its absolute necessity, as taught by Our Lord himself. The law of Baptism applies to all mankind without exception. Unless they are reborn through the grace of Baptism—no matter whether they were born of believing or of unbelieving parents—they are in fact born to eternal misery and loss. The pastor, therefore, must constantly go back to those oft-repeated words of the Gospel: "Unless one is born of water and the Spirit, he cannot enter the kingdom of God," (p. 178).

This is an interesting passage indeed; it allows for *no* exceptions (and "baptisms" of blood and desire are surely exceptions) to the law of baptism. It bears particularly hard on "invincible ignorance," for it will not allow exceptions to be made even for those born (and so presumably raised) with no knowledge of the Faith. This attitude is in keeping with what the Catechism calls the Ultimate Effect of Baptism in N. 58 (p. 191): "...by Baptism the gates of heaven, which sin had closed, are opened to us." It is as simple as that.

Further, this catechism has some rather remarkable things to say with regard to the Church herself:

> 18. The Church is Infallible in Matters of Faith and Morals
> This one Church alone, because it is governed by the Holy Spirit, cannot err in faith or morals (see St. Mt. 28: 16-20). It necessarily follows, furthermore, that all other ecclesial bodies arrogating to themselves the name of "Church," because guided by the spirit of the Devil, fall into the most pernicious errors both doctrinal and moral (see 1 Tim 3:15, 4:1-16). (p. 109).

Strong stuff indeed! But note that it is based firmly on Scripture. If once we admit that in matters spiritual there can be objective truth, then we must admit that all that contradicts the truth is objective falsehood. God being the Spirit of truth, falsehood in such matters reveals the spirit of—whom else? Lest we become unduly ruffled at the implicit accusation that our non-Catholic friends are thus collaborators with the Devil, let us remember that so are we—whenever we sin. It is a common ailment among mankind, though not nearly as dramatic as, say, Satanism.

The next note, which deals with *Figures of the Church of Christ in the Old Testament*, makes particular mention of Noah's Ark. The reason is that "...God has constituted the Church so as to save those who enter her through baptism from all danger of eternal death. Those who are not within her, like those who were not in the Ark, are overwhelmed by their own sins" (*loc. cit.*).

This, then, was the Faith of the Church at the time of the Council of Trent. There were those who believed in Invincible Ignorance, and in Baptism of Desire. But these were for the most part confined to Universities and Seminaries.

In the rest of the Catholic World, tattered and torn by the Protestant Revolt, there was no such quibbling. And what resulted?

The labors of St. Francis Xavier and innumerable others in the Mission fields around the World; the reconquest from the Protestants of large areas they had taken, via such luminaries as St. Francis De Sales and St. Fidelis of Sigmaringen in the Counter-Reformation; outbursts of Mystic fervor in the cloister, producing Saints like Teresa and John of the Cross; rededication in regular diocesan life, as shown by St. Charles Borromeo and St. Thomas of Villanova; and lastly, martyrs—both in Protestant countries as with St. Edmund Campion and St. Edmund Arrowsmith, and Missionary ones, as seen by St. Paul Miki and Bl. Leonard Kimura. In a word, under every conceivable condition, peaceful or not, civilized or not, souls were saved by the millions, and saints produced—which after all is the only real use the Church has.

This was a Faith at once Scriptural, Patristic, and Scholastic, uniting the best of all ages in one synthesis. Despite all appearances to the contrary, it is the Faith of the Church today—although, not of all her placeholders.

For theologians who did not believe these things gradually obtained the upper hand; the ruin we see around us in the Church today is their handiwork, to no small degree. How this came about we shall see in the next chapter.

THE HOUND OF HELL

In a very real sense, the cloister and the Missions are the frontiers of the Church, and the places where, traditionally, the Faith was most fervent. But they are not the centers of the Church; those are Rome and Europe in general. Two major elements contributed to the decay of practical belief in the Church as the Ark of Salvation. One was political and the other philosophical.

The political element was underlined by the Peace of Westphalia in 1648. The Catholic temporal sovereigns of Europe gave up hope of restoring the Protestant realms to Catholic Unity (indeed, France had allied with them); for their Most Christian, Catholic, Faithful, Apostolic, and Orthodox Majesties, co-existence on the basis of national interests became more important than religious uniformity. In time, the Popes came to share this feeling in the political sphere, and this in turn seeped out to the rest of the Church. From political acceptance, personal acceptance was only a matter of time. For (as will be obvious to anyone who knows a great many) there are very many pleasant and, natural speaking, "good" non-Catholics. They like the same sorts of music that we do, or literature, or art. They have stakes in many of the same political battles that we fight. More than that, we number them among our friends or even relatives. In a word, we come to love them; your author no less than any of his readers. "How," we might come to think, "could God condemn such nice folks? Surely He could not be so cruel!" In English-speaking countries, once reconverting Mother England was despaired of, the problem became even more acute. In addition to personal ties much closer than even in Continental countries of mixed religions, there was the need to get along with Protestant neighbors for economic, political, and cultural reasons. What was needed for all concerned was some theological or philosophical way of escaping Traditional Catholic teaching. Such a way presented itself.

As was mentioned in the previous chapter, Thomism carried within it a certain strain of rationalism, taken up from Aristotle. In denying the objective reality of the Universals, it made it difficult to understand how the Fall of Man could affect all Mankind in such an integral manner. While Thomists "saved" this doctrine by saying that because of the Fall all men were born "with an absence of Sanctifying Grace," how could this be if every human was a completely distinct individual? This led leading Thomist philosopher Fr. Frederick Copleston, S.J. to comment "How theologians understand original sin today is not clear to me" (*A History of Medieval Philosophy*, p. 70). Indeed not! Further, as Fr. Coony observed in the last chapter, Nominalism developed out of Moderate Realism and became a leading philosophy before the Reformation. Its adherents, holding that the Universals were mere names, could not be expected to formulate any kind of understanding of Original Sin at all. They must find refuge in the Double Truth. But for them, it would be impossible to understand logically how the Sacraments, mere physical signs, could materially remedy the Fall. It put one in the uncomfortable position of having to believe religiously in rites which one could not actually justify in philosophy. It comes as no surprise that the result of such thinking would be either Luther's flight into Salvation by Faith alone or else Transcendental Thomism's (a la Karl Rahner) Salvation by conduct (or else mere existence) alone. One of the unfortunate by-products of Luther's defection was that in time, with first the decay of Scholasticism and then the rise of Neo-Thomism, Faith's place in Salvation became largely ignored, due in part to "guilt by association" with the "Reformer." So too did Calvin by his distortions, make it difficult for Catholic Theologians to speak of "Predestination" or the "Elect." The Enlightenment, with its emphasis on conduct rather than creed (it is no wonder that Freemasonry, the most notable creation of that era, prides itself on adherence to this shibboleth) added to these developments further. Its assault on Sacramentality as the sole vehicle of Sanctifying Grace was devastating.

But however much the more advanced clerics of the 18th and 19th Centuries might hold these ideas, there were several problems. The liturgies, creeds, prayers, solemn conciliar and papal definitions, writings of Fathers and Saints (with few exceptions), and of course Scripture, still registered the Old Faith once delivered to the Saints. This they could not change. Worse yet, the common people still maintained the old beliefs, as this ballad shows:

> Now sure you know there is but one God
> By Home we are all created
> And sure you know there is but one Faith
> By which we are consecrated;
> And sure you know there is but one Ark
> To keep us from desolation;
> And sure you know there is but one Church
> Can ever expect salvation
> (*Bishop Butler of Kilcash*, anon. Irish, 18th c.)

Luckily for the advanced crew, however, they did have at their disposal the Thomistic love of making distinctions. Now these distinctions do have a certain utility. But unfortunately, they can be used to erode the plain meaning of any given phrase; as Leonard Wibberley observes in *The Mouse That Roared*: yes may be turned to no, or vice versa, provided sufficient verbiage be employed to do so. This has since degenerated into the modern academic sort of criticism. It is a method of analysis which would take the sentence "What do we mean by that?" and ask: "What do we mean by what? What do we mean by do? What do we mean by we?" and so on until one knows less than he did at birth. Applied to the present case, these distinctions allow one to adhere to the ancient dogmas, while avoiding their plain meaning. "Baptism is necessary for Salvation? Of course! Naturally, the vast numbers of people, protected by invincible ignorance, are baptized by desire. No Salvation outside the Church? Certainly! But we need to understand what is meant by Church...or by Outside...or by Salvation." In the end, the whole thing is pared down to meaninglessness, until one can hardly understand why the Church bothered with these things in the first place.

Probably no better commentary can be made on this sort of Neo-Thomism than that of one of the best known Neo-Thomists: Jacques Maritain:

> This "Thomist philosophy" was no theology, since they had withdrawn it from the light proper to theology to transfer it into the kingdom of reason using only its natural powers. Still less was it a philosophy, since it remained structured after the theological treatise from which it emerged, and possessed neither the gait and method, nor the light characteristic of philosophical research. Without the characteristic light of theology, and that proper

philosophical research, it had practically no light at all. (*The Peasant of the Garonne*, p. 136)

This sort of Thomism had the effect of sucking the life out of the Faith; not only did it remove the certainty of the Church's nature and empty her pronouncements on the subject of meaning, it was unable to stand up to Modernism and Americanism. But this is no surprise—these, in a certain sense, were its offspring.

These last did what earlier Liberal-Thomists were unable to do; they—at first slowly, then with increasing speed—made as many alterations in liturgy, prayers, law, and so on as they could. They succeeded in blotting out former solemn pronouncements from the popular mind with the newer ones, proclaiming as development of doctrine what was actually repudiation.

Unfortunately, at every stage of this process, there have been folk who, knowing what the Church actually teaches, have resisted. When such people have been in positions of authority, they have been attacked as tyrants; when not, as contumacious rebels. But of course, authority exists in the Church for the sake of the Faith and the Faithful, and not for private schemes or new religions.

Now then, let us survey the progress made in obscuring the Church's teaching in this matter of Salvation over the last few Centuries.

Fr. William Fannings, S.J., author of the article on Baptism in the *Catholic Encyclopedia*, declares that opposition to baptism of desire was condemned by Pope St. Pius V and Gregory XII, when they condemned the 31st and 33rd propositions of Baius. Since he penned those words, many and many a writer has claimed that every Catholic must believe in baptism of desire, at least in its strict Thomist sense (the Catechumen dying before Baptism). Let us see just what those propositions say:

> 31. Perfect and sincere charity, which is from a "pure heart and good conscience and a faith not feigned" [1 Tim. 1:15], can be in catechumens without remissions of sins. (Denzinger 1031).
>
> 33. A catechumen lives justly and rightly and holily, and observes the commandments of God, and fulfills the law through charity, which is only received in the laver of baptism, before the remission of sins has been obtained. (Denzinger 1033).

All that can be gleaned from these condemnations is that remission of sins—justification—can be obtained by a catechumen prior to baptism. There is nothing here of Salvation for the unbaptized. In any case, there are 79 of these condemned statements, of which Pope St. Pius observes that: "...some could be maintained in some way...", although he objected to the sense in which Baius taught them. Hardly a strong argument there!

It is true, however, that under the influence of some Neo-Thomist philosophers (most notably Suarez) the ideas of baptism of desire and invincible ignorance spread among the clerical intelligentsia. The idea grew up that those who wished to live a moral life, yet were non-Catholic through "no fault of their own," that is, being possessed of invincible ignorance, were somehow members of the Church; if unbaptized, these folk would be saved through baptism of desire. Outside this enormously expanded and amorphous Church, being the well-intentioned company of all who meant well, (as though any but God could determine who means well this side of the grave), of course there was no Salvation! The most advanced seminaries in Europe taught these views, which came to the New World through a former Jesuit, John Carroll, first Archbishop of Baltimore. Indeed, he used practically this very language in "refuting" an anti-Catholic tirade by renegade priest Fr. Charles Wharton. Of course, Carroll also favored election of bishops and a vernacular liturgy. At any rate, these ideas allowed Carroll to initiate the policy of shedding anything Catholic which differentiated the Faithful in the U.S. from their non-Catholic neighbors. There was an interesting method of missionizing! Become just like the natives, and then they won't need to convert! There is little of the Gospel in all of this, but much of the social climber.

But orthodox voices were not lacking then either. St. Alphonsus Liguori (1696—1787), founder of the Redemptorists, bishop of Sant' Agatha dei Goti, author of innumerable books of moral and dogmatic theology as well as devotion, was a consummate mystic. Because of his teaching about Our Lady and the Blessed Sacrament he has been made a Doctor of the Church. During his lifetime he suffered many things, at one point being deposed from headship of his order by the Pope as a result of conspiracy by his closest collaborators. Yet to him belongs one of the most spectacular instances of bilocation, as he appeared to attend Clement XIV at his deathbed even while in a church in his diocese. His writings on the topic at hand are voluminous. In his commentary on the Council of Trent, he informs us that:

> When we say that faith is necessary for the remission of sins, we mean to speak of the Catholic faith, not heretical faith... Without the habit of this faith, no man is justified.

In regard to baptism he says:

> It should be known that Baptism is not only the first but also the most necessary of all the Sacraments. Without Baptism, no one can enter Heaven (*Preaching of God's Word*, 512).

Very definite, indeed. But what of invincible ignorance? He does indeed have an answer:

> How thankful we ought to be to Jesus Christ for the gift of faith! What would have become of us if we had been born in Asia, Africa, America, or in the midst of heretics and schismatics? He who does not believe is lost. This, then, was the first and greatest grace bestowed on us: our calling to the true faith. O Saviour of the world, what would have become of us if Thou hadst not enlightened us? We would have been like our fathers of old, who adored animals and blocks of stone and wood; and thus we would have all perished. (P*reparation for Death,* 339).

Who, then, was correct? Carroll or Liguori? Which of the two was more devoted to the unchanging teachings of the Church, which was the saintlier, which was the greater apostle? Which was made a Doctor of the Church? But we need not guess. In 1786, a group of Tuscan bishops gathered at Pistoia in order to introduce various errors into Italy. This called forth from Pius VI an Apostolic Constitution, *Auctorem fidei*, in which 85 of the propositions passed by the Synod of Pistoia were condemned. Number 26 concerns us most closely:

> The doctrine which rejects as a Pelagian fable, that place of the lower regions (which the faithful generally designate as the limbo of children) in which the souls of those departing with the sole guilt of original sin are punished with the punishment of the condemned, exclusive of the punishment of fire, just as if, by this

very fact, that those who remove the punishment of fire introduced that middle place and state free of guilt and of punishment between the kingdom of God and eternal damnation, such as that about which the Pelagians idly talk,—rash, false, and injurious to Catholic schools. (Denzinger 1526)

It is rather intriguing that a condemnation issued against an opposite heresy—that infants suffer the torment of Hell—should be applicable here. But that is how the truth becomes known. For this condemnation merely repeats the teaching of Innocent III centuries earlier, that deprivation of God is the result of Original Sin, and the torments of Hell the punishment for actual sin.

And, as Archbishop George Hay wrote in 1787,

...if even the children of Christian parents, who die without baptism, cannot go to heaven, how much less can those go there, who, besides being never baptized, are supposed, in the present case, to live and die in the ignorance of the true God, or of Jesus Christ and His faith, and, on that account, must also be supposed to have committed many actual sins themselves (*The Sincere Christian*, "Enquiry: Is there Salvation Outside the Catholic Church?," Qu. 7).

So then, on the eve of the French Revolution, which will quiet doctrinal debate until 1815, we have two theories regarding the dogma, "Outside the Church there is no Salvation." The first, held by Pius VI, St. Alphonsus Liguori, and Archbishop Hay (among others), with the Scriptures, Fathers and Doctors, Popes and Councils behind them on the one side, holding that the words mean what they say, and a dessicated Neo-Thomist claiming that they do not, held by Carroll and other avant-garde clerics, presumably including the English Jesuits who had taught him in France, on the other. Europe might be still open to the old teaching, but the accession of Carroll to the See of Baltimore meant that the second team would be dominant in the new United States. When these were a poor struggling country, and their Catholics insignificant on the world Church scene, this might have counted for little. But that situation would change.

Meanwhile, back in Europe, the privations of war led many back to the Faith; much of the Romantic Revival produced many converts. Some of these, enthralled purely by the beauty of the

Church and fueled by their emotions, were extremely imprecise in their dogmatic notions: indeed, in Protestant circles, Romantics like Schliermacher became positively anti-dogmatic. But the same impulse led others to rediscover the intellectual heritage of the Middle Ages. Some of these became quite dogmatic indeed.

Even among cradle Catholics, the concrete demonstration of Man's fallen nature which they received through such Revolutionary activities as the Terror led many to abandon the rationalistic liberalism which gave intellectual birth to such as John Carroll. Gone was the naïve optimism of the Enlightenment. In its place was a clear-eyed realization of the truths of existing circumstances.

Among the foremost of the Romantic Catholic philosophers and theologians was the great German, Franz von Baader (1765-1841). Trained as a mining engineer, he nevertheless had a great attraction to Mystical theology. Rediscovering the heritage of the Ultra-Realist philosophers, he retired from mining in 1820. Six years later, he became professor of philosophy and speculative theology at Munich. From then until his death, he elaborated in diverse writing (coming to 16 volumes) his philosophy, which touches upon everything from the State to Science to Dogma. Summarizing his teaching on the matter at hand, one authority puts it: "The means whereby we put ourselves so in relation with Christ as to receive from Him His healing virtue are chiefly prayer and the sacraments of the Church; mere works are never sufficient." In this he revolted against the "conduct first" attitude of the Enlightenment and of the Neo-Thomists as well. To him is often given credit for spearheading the Scholastic Revival of the 19th Century, yet his insistence on returning to Scholasticism in its pre-Suaresian manifestations led him into conflict with the clergy, although the troubles were of short duration.

Another such was Joseph De Maistre (1754-1821). Known today primarily as a political philosopher, he was also a profound writer on religious topics. He was in fact a vigorous defender both of the necessity of the Church and Papal Infallibility.

But these ideas were not confined to lay intellectuals. Ven. William Joseph Chaminade, born in 1761, continued to minister to his flock throughout the Revolution, although he was often hunted. After peace returned, he founded the Society of Mary (Marists), an order of brothers dedicated to teaching. He was considered a very holy man in his lifetime, and he combined holiness with great learning (hence his love of teaching). What does he have to say on the topic of Salvation?

> The union of Christ with the members of the Mystical Body is obtained only by members in the Church, for outside this chaste spouse there is no union with the Bridegroom. She alone has the advantages of this divine union, and she alone has received the keys which are a mark of the power attached to the union. She alone is united to the Bridegroom, and she alone possesses the fecundity which is the fruit of this union. There is no life outside the Church because all the life that is to be had can come only from her. Outside the Church there is no Salvation. (*Mary in our Christ-Life*, 47).
>
> Since our lamentable fall in the Garden of Eden, faith in Jesus Christ has been indispensably necessary for salvation, so that whoever has not believed in Him has not been saved. (*op. cit., 122)*

The 19th Century also had its wonder-working Saints, as many as in any other era of the Church. One of these was the great Apostle of the Eucharist, St. Peter Julian Eymard (1811-1868). After laboring for a while as a parish priest, he joined the Marist order. Eventually, he founded his own Society of the Blessed Sacrament for priests, and an order of nuns dedicated to Perpetual Adoration. He wrote a long series of books on Eucharistic and Marian devotion, which breathe a spirit of purest Catholicism. What was his view?

> Jesus Christ is given to us through the Church, just as He was given to the Church through Mary... The Church alone has received the deposit of Faith in Jesus Christ... and it is through the Holy Catholic Church alone that men can become true children of the faith... Unfortunate are the nations that do not live in the Church of Jesus Christ. They are like men outside the Ark at the time of the Flood. Outside the Church, these poor travelers wander without a guide in the desert. They are like a sailor on a boat without either rudder or pilot. Alas, unfortunate children, abandoned on the road, without a mother to nourish and love them; they will soon die of cold and hunger! The gift of the Church as our mother and teacher in the Faith is therefore the greatest grace Jesus Christ could bestow upon us. And the greatest charity we can do to a man is to lead him to the true Church, outside which there is no Salvation. (*Eucharistic Handbook*, 136-137).

Great as the fame of St. Peter Julian Eymard has been, a friend of his has gained even greater: St. John Marie Vianney (1786-1859), the Curé d'Ars. After his 1925 canonization he was declared patron of parish priests four years later. His miracles are very well known: how he could tell penitents their sins; how through the intercession of St. Philomena (to whom he was devoted) he performed the multiplication of loaves and fishes; how he was visibly persecuted by demons; and many other wonderful things. Fewer know how much trouble he had in seminary, nor that in the beginning his people at Ars worked against him. But through personal holiness, he triumphed over all, and received penitents from all classes and all European countries. In a word, he was the Padre Pio of his time (save that he had no stigmata; the latter was the first priest ever to receive it). He says:

> My children, why are there no Sacraments in other religions? Because there is no salvation there! We have the Sacraments at our disposal because we belong to the religion of salvation. We are bound to give thanks to God for them from our hearts, for the Sacraments are the sources of salvation. It is not so in other religions. (quoted in *The Apostolic Digest*, 269)

The good curé wrote much more along those lines. Personally loving and kind to all, he was nevertheless a stickler for doctrine. So too was St. Anthony Mary Claret, the only canonized Father of Vatican I. He wrote: "He who is not with Peter is not with the Church, and he who leaves the Ark will perish in the flood." He was, of course, yet another latter-day wonder-worker.

It may be objected at this point that, in the course of the 19th Century, many seminaries in Europe as well as America taught the contrary to what these Saints believed—and did so with the authority of their dioceses or orders. To this your author must reply that, just as many of these institutions were infected in the 18th Century with Jansenism, Gallicanism, Josephinism, and Febronianism, so were they in the 19th Century afflicted with a host of errors: Rosminianism, Hermesianism, Guntherianism, and strongest of all, Liberalism, which in its root claimed that the Church had no authority over the State; indeed, no authority at all, save over consciences. Its credo was "a free Church in a free State," tending toward religious equality for all faiths whether true or false. If asked whether or not the Church was the sole Ark of Salvation (and so deserved special rights from the State), they inevitably took refuge in SS. Ambrose, Augustine, and Thomas Aquinas, as well as that single passage of Trent. Despite repeated condemnations, these ideas grew and festered in secret, if not openly. Many American priests (such as the later Archbishop Ireland) were infected by them, returning to an environment ready-made for such beliefs by the teachings of Carroll and his compadres.

But what of official Church teachings? Many modern theologians would discount the writings we have quoted as being "merely devotional," as though piety had one truth and scholarship another (but then, that is the Double Truth, isn't it?). Pope Gregory XVI (1831-1846) before his election to the Papacy had been a Camaldolese monk (an extremely austere order). His very first Encyclical, *Summo iugiter studio*, issued in 1832, dealt with the question:

> You know how zealously Our predecessors taught that very article of faith which these dare to deny, namely the necessity of the Catholic faith and of unity for salvation. The words of that celebrated disciple of the apostles, martyred St. Ignatius, in his letter to the Philadelphians are relevant to this matter: "Be not deceived, my brother; if anyone follows a schismatic, he will not attain the inheritance of the kingdom of God." Moreover, St. Augustine and the other African bishops who met in the Council of Cirta in the year 412 explained the same thing at greater length: "Whoever has separated himself from the Catholic Church, no matter how laudably he lives, will not have eternal life, but has earned the anger of God because of this one crime: that he abandoned his union with Christ." Omitting other appropriate passages which are almost numberless in the writings of the Fathers, We shall praise St. Gregory the Great who expressly testifies that this is indeed the teaching of the Catholic Church. He says: "The holy universal Church teaches that it is not possible to worship God truly except in her and asserts that all who are outside of her will not be saved." Official acts of the Church proclaim the same dogma. Thus, in the decree on faith which Innocnent III published with the synod of Lateran IV, these things are written: "There is one universal Church of the faithful outside of which no one is saved." Finally, the same dogma is also expressly mentioned in the profession of faith proposed by the Apostolic See, not only that which all Latin churches use, but also that which the Greek Orthodox Church uses and that which other Eastern Catholics use... We are so concerned about this serious

and well-known dogma, which has been attacked with such remarkable audacity, that We could not restrain Our pen from reinforcing this truth with many testimonies.

Strive to eradicate these slithering errors with all your strength. Inspire the populace... to keep the Catholic faith and unity as the only way of salvation with an ever more ardent zeal, and thus, to avoid every danger of forsaking it. (Caps. 5-6)

In this he repeated the words of his short-lived predecessor, Pius VIII (1829-1830), in the latter's single encyclical, *Traditi Humiliati*; and of Leo XII (1823-1829) in *Ubi primum*. Gregory reiterated this teaching in the same year in *Mirari vos*. Despite his warnings, however, the opposite teaching continued to grow in "enlightened" Catholic circles, both clerical and lay.

In 1846, Pius IX ascended the Papal throne; believing him to be one of their own, the Liberals rejoiced. Indeed, although experience (like being chased from Rome in 1848, and losing the City in 1870) later taught him otherwise, at first he seemed to justify their hopes. Even after his opinions changed, however, he retained perhaps some small residue of his former intellectual disposition. However that may be, he did at least issue three documents over which opponents of the Church's traditional teaching on Salvation rejoiced. One was the text of an allocution, *Singulari quadem*, on 9 December 1854. An excerpt of this allocution was, prior to Vatican II, inevitably quoted in Liberal books on this subject: "...it is equally certain that those who are ignorant of the true religion, if that ignorance is invincible, will not be held guilty in the matter..." This is generally taken to mean that as long as anyone "can't" know about the Faith, he will be saved. But of course, however much this passage is quoted, it really ought to be quoted in full:

> For, it must be held by faith that outside the Apostolic Roman Church, no one can be saved; that this is the only ark of salvation; that he who shall not have entered therein will perish in the flood; but on the other hand, it is necessary to hold for certain that those who labour in ignorance of the true religion, if this ignorance is invincible, are not stained by guilt in this matter in the eyes of God. Now, in truth, who would arrogate so much to himself as to mark the limits of such an ignorance, because of the nature and variety of people, regions, innate dispositions, and of so many other things? For in truth, when released from these corporeal chains "we shall see God as He is", we shall understand perfectly

by how close a bond divine mercy and justice are united; but, as long as we are on earth, weighed down by this mortal mass which blunts the soul, let us hold most firmly, that, in accordance with Catholic teaching, there is "one God, one faith, one baptism;" it is unlawful to proceed further in enquiry. (Denzinger 1647).

It should be readily apparent here that there is no question of "invincible" ignorance being salvific; merely that if it is truly "invincible" (and His Holiness confesses himself incapable of saying much beyond that) it absolves the individual from the guilt of the specific sin of refusing to join the Church. This is not the same thing as saying such a one will be saved thereby. I may never have murdered in my life; but if I die in Original sin with my customary actual sins—unregenerate and unshriven—I cannot enter into the kingdom of God. But as we have seen in the last chapter, all sorts of strange things happen in the process of drawing the good-willed into the Church, most of which we will know nothing about while alive. So we must hold to the Traditional teachings of the Church, leaving aside all speculation on the matter. That this is the view to be taken of this allocution may be proven by two things: one, that it must be taken that way if it is to square with the writings of the predecessors; and two, that in the previous paragraph of the same allocution, he condemns the opinion that "one should have good hope of the eternal salvation of all those who have never lived in the true Church of Jesus Christ." (Denzinger 1646). Needless to say, were he actually presenting an innovation in contradiction to past teachings (as indeed, some Popes, e.g. John XXII) have done, it would have to be ignored. The more so because an allocution is a mere private address delivered by the Pope in Consistory to the Cardinals, although it may be published later if the subject is of general interest, as this one was. As such, it is not protected by infallibility.

Something of a tougher nut to crack is Pius IX's local encyclical to the bishops of Italy, *Quanto conficiamur*. Therein he wrote, much to the glee of later Liberals:

> ...We should mention again and censure a very grave error in which some Catholics are unhappily engaged, who believe that men living in error, and separated from the true faith and from Catholic unity, can attain eternal life. Indeed, this is certainly quite contrary to Catholic teaching. It is known to Us and to you that

> they who labor in invincible ignorance of our most holy religion and who, zealously keeping the natural law and its precepts engraved in the hearts of all by God, and being ready to obey God, live an honest and upright life, can, by the operating power of divine light and grace, attain eternal life, since God who clearly beholds, searches, and knows the minds, souls, thoughts, and habits of all men, because of His great goodness and mercy, will by no means suffer anyone to be punished with eternal torment who has not the guilt of deliberate sin. But, the Catholic dogma that no one can be saved outside the Catholic Church is well known... (Denzinger 1677).

This too was often quoted as though it changed the entirety of Church teaching; indeed, a superficial reading can give that impression. Alas, no such luck. Obviously, since Pius has just reiterated that one cannot save his soul outside the Church, he is speaking here of precisely the same sorts of odd occurrences we have previously looked at in the Missions. If men are of Good Will, God will indeed enlighten them; how, we will not always find out. The Pope goes on to say that those not "guilty of the stain of deliberate sin," will not suffer eternal torment. Here we are reminded of the distinction between the torments reserved for actual sin, and the absence of God which is the result of Original Sin. But who amongst us adults is not guilty of the stain of deliberate sin? So we see again, that Pope Pius is not proposing that Invincible Ignorance is salvific, although this is often misquoted as "ignorance of the true faith, if it be invincible, excuses one from all fault in the eyes of the Saviour." Of course, even if it did state this, a local encyclical carries no weight in propounding innovations contrary to received teaching—which this was not.

That the interpretation here put forth is the correct one will be obvious not only from the texts themselves, prior teaching, and Pope Pius IX's other writings. Most particularly, we may point out the *Syllabus of Errors*, which condemns the following propositions:

> 16. Men can, in the cult of any religion, find the way of eternal salvation and attain eternal salvation...
> 17. One ought to at least have good hope for the eternal salvation of all those who in no way dwell in the true Church of Christ...

18. Protestantism is nothing else than a different form of the same religion, in which, equally as in the Catholic Church, it is given to please God...

Not at all what the misinterpreters of his allocution and local encyclical would have us believe, are they? Moreover, some claim, due to their universal nature, the condemnations of the Syllabus may even be Infallible. It is notable that of all the words he employed in his 9 December 1854 allocution, of which so much has been made by so many only the condemnation of proposition 17 was thought fit by him to promulgate universally. What, then, was Pius IX's personal view? We must assume that it was the same as his official, as this story related in his biography by Fr. Francis Thornton suggests:

> A group of Church of England clerics, who were at least technically heretics, *insisted* to the Pope that there must be some form of blessing he could properly give them "There is," replied the Holy Father, and he used the words of the celebrant at High Mass when he blesses the incense: "*Ab illo benedicaris in cuius honore cremaberis.*" (May you be blessed by Him in whose honor you will be burned). (*Cross Upon Cross*, p. 214)

Yet, despite—or actually because of—his zeal for the Church as the sole means of salvation, he counseled Catholics not to be hostile to those outside the Church,

> ...but rather they should always be zealous to seek them out and aid them, whether poor, or sick, or afflicted with any other burdens, with all the offices of Christian charity; and they should endeavor especially to snatch them from the darkness of error in which they unhappily lie, and lead them back to Catholic truth...so that...they may attain eternal salvation (Denzinger 1678).

He is a Venerable, has quite a number of posthumous miracles, and may be canonized one day. It would not be too surprising, for a combination of unsparing fervor and rectitude in matters of doctrine, combined with authentic kindness and charity in conduct, have ever marked the Saints whatever the disparities of their personalities. This is as it should be, for these two qualities are in the end the same.

Nor will we find his next four successors teaching otherwise. There is much we could quote from each of them. But a short one apiece should suffice—so here goes:

Leo XIII: "This is the order of God: salvation is to be found nowhere but in the Church" (*Annum ingress sumus*, in *Papal Teachings: The Church*, no. 653, selected by the Benedictines of Solesmes).

St. Pius X: "It is our duty to recall to everyone, great and small, the absolute necessity we are under to have recourse to this Church in order to work out our eternal salvation" (*Jucunda sane, ibid, no. 668*).

Benedict XV: "In Holy Mother Church lies all hope of eternal salvation... if anyone is outside the Ark of Noah, he will perish in the overwhelming flood" (*Spiritus paraclitus*, in *Rome and the Study of Scripture*).

Lastly, we have Pius XI: "If any man does not enter the Church, or if any man departs from it, he is far from the hope of life and salvation" (*Mortalium animos*, cap. 11).

Doubtless, if Papal pronouncements were all that Catholic theologians went by, this would not be a question.

But unfortunately, such was not the case. To combat Liberalism, Leo XIII gave particular patronage to Neo-Thomism, which under the circumstances is quite understandable. But attempting to retain their customary misreadings of Ss. Ambrose, Augustine, and Thomas gave an important segment of the most orthodox clerics a real stake in trying to square the circle: how to reconcile the dogma of "Outside the Church there is no Salvation" —buttressed as we have seen with all sorts of solemn and infallible pronouncements—with the goal of somehow admitting non-Catholics to a sort of honorary membership, and so allowing them to be saved without being Catholic. Logically, it is an impossible task; it can only be done by distorting language itself, giving new and unheard-of meanings to words. This insidious process with regard to the doctrine of salvation was well called "slithering error" by Gregory XVI, for that is precisely its mode of operation.

Trained in this sort of discourse, those who later became the Americanists and the Modernists honed it to a fine art. St. Pius X described well their thought patterns in *Pascendi* (Denzinger 2078):

> [For the Modernists] the mind operates in a twofold way: first, by a natural and spontaneous act it presents the matter in a simple and popular judgment; but then after reflection and deeper consideration, or, by *elaborating the thought*, as they say, it speaks forth its thoughts in *secondary* judgments, derived, to be sure, from the simple first, but more precise and distinct. These *secondary* judgments, if they are finally sanctioned by the supreme magisterium of the Church, will constitute dogma.

For many ecclesiastics, otherwise orthodox, this method had already been used in regard to Salvation: had not Trent approved baptism of desire and Pius IX invincible ignorance? They were off and slithering! But the great feat of the Modernists was to apply the same method to every other dogma (and in our own time to every strictly moral teaching), and nuance them all out of existence.

St. Pius X gave the Modernists something of a thrashing. Under Benedict XV the *Sodalitium Pianum* (a semi-clandestine organization of clerics and laity concerned with ferreting out Modernists), their major nemesis, was done away with, and they finally began to emerge during World War II. Vatican II saw them circle in for the kill, with the aftermath being the vultures picking the Mystical Body as clean as they could. But we shall return to Europe and Rome presently. For now, let us cross back over to the Americas in the early 19th Century.

CATHOLICISM IN AMERICA

Latin America was torn throughout that Century first by the Wars of Independence, and then by the struggles of pro-clerical Conservatives and anti-clerical Liberals, the latter aided by the United States. But to show the beliefs of the people in the first half of the century, Venezuelan Liberal strongman Francisco Santander felt compelled to reassure his subjects in 1836: "I love my religion because I live happily in it, and know that outside the Catholic Church there is no eternal Salvation" (J. Lloyd Mecham, *Church and State in Latin America*, p. 144).

In the United States, however, things were different. Carroll's teachings were somewhat dissipated in the next generation because of the enormous numbers of immigrants that came over from Europe, still believing the Catholic faith of their Fathers. With them came many clerics and religious, and a few bishops. Yet Carrollism would remain as a powerful undercurrent in American Church life, only to re-emerge after the Civil War as Americanism.

But such immigrants as St. John Neumann, Bishop of Philadelphia, were unaffected by it. A Redemptorist, he followed closely in teachings and life, the example of St. Alphonsus Liguori, the founder of his order. After his death (as before) miracles were ascribed to him, and his tomb is even today a place of pilgrimage; a friend of your author's had a cancer which went into remission following a trip to the bishop's resting-place. St. John Neumann had very strong ideas on the question of salvation: "The unbaptized, therefore, being in a state of sin, must necessarily be baptized if they wish to please God and be saved." He wrote much else about the necessity of the Sacraments for salvation, but most telling of all are the relevant questions in his *Small Catechism of the Christian Religion* first composed in the 1840s, and one of the two most popular until Cardinal Gibbons issued his *Baltimore Catechism* four decades later.

In the section on Baptism, we see:

> Q. 3. Why is Baptism the most necessary Sacrament?
> A. Because without Baptism no one can be saved.
> Q. 4. Why can we not be saved without Baptism?
> A. Because we are cleansed from original sin only by Baptism.
> Q. 6. What effect has Baptism on man?
> A. He is made a child of God, an heir of Heaven, and a Christian.

The section on the Church informs us:

> Q. 12. Can we be saved in every religion?
> A. No, we can be saved only in the religion that Jesus Christ has taught.
> Q. 13. Where do we find this religion of Jesus Christ?
> A. We find it in the Roman Catholic Church.

Interestingly enough, the other best-selling Catechism, Fr. Deharbe's, answers the question "Will any Faith save us?" with "No; only the true Faith which the Catholic Church teaches, will save us." The next query, "Why has the Catholic Church alone the truth Faith," receives the reply "Because the Catholic Church alone received its Faith from Christ, and has always kept it incorrupt." The questions on Baptism were practically identical to Neumann's.

Nor was the old religion restricted to immigrants; many native-born Americans received it also. One of the most distinguished of the early converts was Orestes Brownson (1803-1876), a former New England Transcendentalist, and colleague of Channing, Emerson, Hawthorne, and the rest. He published *Brownson's Quarterly Review* from his conversion in 1844 until within three years of his death. He did his best to overcome both his upbringing and the proto-Americanism of his time. Upon moving to New York in 1855, however, he fell in with Isaac Hecker, a convert who would later be expelled from the Redemptorists, and with those who would be the first members of his new order, the Paulists. Their method of conversion consisted of presenting "only so much of Catholic doctrine to those not Catholic as was absolutely necessary for them to accept in order to enter the Church..." (Henry Brownson, *Latter Life*, p. 262). The next year, Bishop John Hughes attacked this policy. During later life, Brownson wrote of his collaboration with these men that:

> The only trouble I have grows out of the fact that Fr. Hewitt is not sound on the question of original sin, and does not believe that it is necessary to be in communion with the Church in order to be saved. He holds that Protestants may be saved by invincible ignorance, and that original sin was no sin at all except the individual sin of Adam, and that our nature was not wounded at all by it. Fr. Hecker agrees with him on these points, and is in fact a semi-Pelagian without knowing it. So I am obliged to abstain [as an employee on the Paulist magazine] from bringing out what I regard as the orthodox doctrine of original sin and of exclusive salvation. (Brownson, *op. cit.,* 565-566).

Brownson realized after long years that soft-pedaling would not serve the cause of the Church. Toward the end of his life, he wrote in *Brownson's Quarterly Review* ("Answer to Objections," July 1874, pp. 413-414; *Works,* XX, 413-414):

> There can be no more fatal mistake than to soften, liberalize, or latitudinize this terrible dogma, "Out of the Church there is no Salvation" ... If we wish to convert Protestants and infidels we must preach in all its rigor the naked dogma. Give them the smallest peg, or what appears so, not to you, but to them; —the smallest peg, on which to hand a hope of salvation without being in or actually reconciled to the Church by the Sacrament of Penance, and all the arguments you can address to them to prove the necessity of being in the Church in order to be saved will have no more effect on them than rain on a duck's back.

But whatever realizations Brownson had come to, these were not shared by his erstwhile Paulist collaborators. They continued their own version of "evangelization."

Meanwhile, the year after Brownson penned the just quoted words, a book appeared with the *imprimatur* of the then Archbishop of Baltimore, Roosevelt Bayley (nephew of St. Elizabeth Seton). *Familiar Explanation of Christian Doctrine* was arranged as a catechism. It contained what by our standards are extremely inflammatory statements:

> Q. Who then will be saved?
> A. Christ has solemnly declared that only those will be saved who have done God's will on earth as explained, not by private interpretation, but by the infallible teaching of the Roman Catholic Church.

> Q. But is it not a very uncharitable doctrine to say that no one can be saved out of the Church?
>
> A. On the contrary, it is a very great act of charity to assert most emphatically, that out of the Catholic Church there is no salvation possible; for Jesus Christ and His Apostles have taught this doctrine in very plain language...

Who wrote this way? Fr. Michael Mueller, CSsR., a Redemptorist priest; who indeed, at the time of this book's appearance, was one of the most popular and widely-read theological writers in Catholic America.

Fr. Mueller was born in Germany in 1825; after joining the Redemptorists, he was sent to Philadelphia, where he was ordained by St. John Neuman in 1853. Under that prelate, he served in many capacities, and began his writing career in the mid-1860s. He eventually authored over 35 books. Like his superior, he firmly held the doctrine regarding salvation. Unlike the Paulists, he was quite willing to apply it to the contemporary American scene:

> Q. Have Protestants any faith in Christ?
> A. They never had.
> Q. Why not?
> A. Because there never lived any such a Christ as they imagine and believe in.
> Q. In what kind of Christ do they believe?
> A. In such a one whom they can make a liar with impunity, whose doctrines they can interpret as they please, and who does not care what a man believes, provided he be an honest man before the public.
> Q. Will such a faith in such a Christ save Protestants?
> A. No sensible man will assert such an absurdity.
> Q. What follows from this?
> A. That they die in their sins and are damned.

Before we moderns express our horror at this last line, it is important to remember that Fr. Mueller, echoing all the prior teaching we have looked at, did not say that anyone who had ever been a Protestant was damned. But as he points out in the article *Questions and Answers on Salvation*, also written in 1875 (qu. 41):

> If we sincerely do not wish to make great mistakes in explaining the great revealed truth, "Out of the Church there is no

Salvation," we must remember: 1. That there are four great truths of salvation, which everyone must know and believe in order to be saved; 2. That no one can go to Heaven unless he is in the state of sanctifying grace; 3. That, in order to receive sanctifying grace, the soul must be prepared for it by divine Faith, Hope, Charity, the true sorrow for sin with the firm purpose of doing all that God requires the soul to believe and to do, in order to be saved; 4. That this preparation of the soul cannot be brought about by inculpable ignorance. And if such ignorance cannot even dispose the soul for receiving the grace of justification, it can much less give this grace to the soul. Inculpable ignorance has never been a means of grace or salvation, not even for the inculpably ignorant people that live up to their conscience.

Elsewhere in the book cited, as a result of this teaching, Fr. Mueller tells us that we cannot speculate as to who does or does not die in their sins, since no one "knows what passes between God and the souls of men at the moment of death." Here we see again, the question of Good Will.

In 1888, the *Familiar Explanation* was attacked by the Episcopalian (Anglican) bishop of Western New York, Arthur C. Coxe, as proof of the Church's "false" teachings. In reply, the Paulist *Buffalo Catholic Union and Times* in their 26 January 1888 issue carried an anonymous article declaring that Mueller had misrepresented the Church's teaching, and that "Protestants believe precisely what Catholics believe about Christ." (Your author can only ask: which Protestants? Certainly, most do not believe that He transubstantiates; fewer still that He appointed Peter to be head of the Church).

The same journal, in its 22 March 1888 edition, attacked Mueller again, in an article entitled: "Have Protestants Divine Faith?" Written by a Paulist Priest, Fr. Alfred Young, the article asserted that the

> ...actual faith of Protestants, who are in good faith, is identical with ours in its essential quality... I was once a Protestant, and my faith was just as truly and theologically divine as it is today... and in becoming a Catholic it underwent no change, and plainly could not undergo any.

Still, your author is intemperate enough to wish that it had, since the good Fr. Young mentions elsewhere in the article that part of his "truly and theologically divine" Protestant faith had been

> ...that the Roman Catholic Church was the church of anti-Christ, that she was the scarlet woman of Babylon and the Pope the man of sin; that she taught false doctrines; that she was the great enemy of all Christian truth, morality, and love of God.

He then concludes with the stirring assertion that if only a man be sincere in his beliefs,

> ...that man is a Catholic in the sight of God, and he is a Catholic in the sight of the Church, no matter what he calls himself, and though one dies piously as an Episcopalian, Presbyterian, Methodist, Baptist, or what not, St. Peter will let him into Heaven as a Catholic.

Given all of this, one wonders why Fr. Young bothered to "convert."

Fr. Mueller's reply was a book, *The Catholic Dogma: Outside the Church There is Positively no Salvation*, published by Benziger Brothers in July 1888. In his introduction, Fr. Mueller wrote:

> Now is it not something very shocking to see such condemned errors and perverse opinions proclaimed as Catholic doctrine in a Catholic Newspaper, and in books written and recently published by Catholics? We have, therefore, deemed it our duty to make a strong, vigorous, and uncompromising presentation of the fundamental truth, the very fence and barrier of the true religion, "OUTSIDE OF THE CHURCH THERE IS POSITIVELY NO SALVATION," against those soft, weak, timid, liberalizing Catholics, who labor to explain away all the points of Catholic Faith offensive to non-Catholics, and to make it appear that there is no question of life and death, of heaven and hell, involved in the differences between us and the Protestants.

The book is a compendious collection of the writings of the Fathers and Doctors on the question, and establishes their practical unanimity in favor of the traditional position. Mueller sums up their position as "Heretics are out of the Roman Catholic Church; therefore, if they die as heretics, they are lost forever."

The August 1888 issue of the Paulist New York based magazine, *The Catholic World*, contained an attack on Mueller's latest work by another Paulist, Fr. Walter Elliot. Mueller replied, challenging them to debate via letter with him in another lay-run (and so presumably neutral) Catholic paper, *The New York Freeman's Journal*. From 15 September to 1 December 1888, letters went back and forth in that publication's pages, with Mueller on one side, and Elliot and Young on the other. Most of these were much as we have seen: Young and Elliot treating sentimental expressions as authoritative Church teaching, and Mueller replying with Patristic and Magisterial pronouncements.

On 29 September, Mueller charged that his Paulist opponents rewrote the doctrine under discussion:

> ... to mean anything else but what the words literally imply... Out of the Catholic Church there is positively no salvation. This is a truth revealed by God to His Church like any other Catholic dogma, and most assuredly He knows whom He does and whom He does not let into Heaven. In our work, we have furnished every Catholic with the best weapons to defend the great truth in question, which was never called in question in any century except ours, in which liberal-minded Catholics and such converts as were received into the Church without having the gift of faith, have tried to explain away the great dogma, or make believe that certain men belonged to the Church who never belonged to it, and are saved by invincible ignorance.

The controversy ground on. Many priests and laymen wrote in to the editor applauding Mueller's stand, and expressing their relief that someone was standing up for the doctrine. Among those convinced by Mueller's arguments was the editor, James McMaster. Himself a convert, McMaster was an early friend of Fr. Hecker, and had in fact gone with him to try his vocation in Belgium. But finding himself called to the lay state, he took over the paper in 1853, editing it until his death in 1907. He ranks with Brownson as one of the two great American lay Apostles of the 19th Century.

But however much support Mueller may have garnered from an open audience with few prejudices, such was not the case with his own order. Much had changed since Mueller's mentor, St. John Neumann, had steered both the Archdiocese of Philadelphia and the Redemptorist Order in the U.S. Fr. Schauer, the Redemptorist

Provincial, ordered Mueller to cease the controversy. He thought of writing Fr. Nicholas Mauron, the Superior General of the Order, about the Mueller affair, but before he could, Mauron wrote him. Seizing upon Mueller's use of strong language against his opponents (in desperation, after they refused to refute his points), the Superior General deplored Mueller's use of invective and commanded Schauer "that he [Mueller] be forbidden to engage in this form of polemics."

Of course, given Fr. Mueller's bluff temperament, and his opponents' refusal to attempt refutation of the evidences he presented, his giving way to use of "dishonest," "liars," "heretics," and "unCatholic" in addressing them may be understood. Today, of course, such lapses are not permitted in religious debate, which is in any case not considered to encompass truths (or falsehoods) worth getting angry over. But politics are still considered to have some objective worth, and so name-calling is still permitted in that sphere. If ever they too at last become irrelevant, it may be understood that the most rigid courtesy will be incarnate in discussions of abstract political principles—principles which in any case will have no real relationship to actual living, just as religious ones do not in our day.

At any rate, Schauer carried out Mauron's orders, paying a visit to the Paulist Superior, Fr. Deshon. The two agreed that Mueller was to cease immediately, and the Paulists would have the last word in Fr. Young's 1 December article; the incident would then be considered closed, without, of course, any actual conclusion reached. Naturally, the Paulists did not keep their side of the bargain, following up Young's parting shot with a scathing review of *The Catholic Dogma* by Fr. Elliot. But then, what use *is* an agreement, if it limits you? Even so, Fr. Mueller was not allowed to reply.

He was further forbidden to write any more articles at all. But he continued to publish and market successive printings of *The Catholic Dogma*. In these years, the doctrinal and cultural feud between the Americanist (Gibbons, Ireland, the Paulists, etc.) and the Ultra-Montanes or Conservatives (Corrigan, McQuaid, many of the Catholic non-English speaking clerics and laity) heated up. The battles went back and forth—on public schools, ethnic parishes and bishops, inter-faith worship, Fr. Hecker's and the Paulist's methods, and on and on. During all this time, Fr. Mueller's book gave much assistance to the enemies of the Americanists.

As has been noted earlier, the Americanists were not without friends in Rome, most notably the Secretary of State, Cardinal Rampolla. The fighting would go from episode to episode, with the Americanists attempting to destroy traditional teachings and structures, while their opponents would defend them. The strategies of both parties included getting the ear of the increasingly debilitated Leo XIII, and securing his actions on the particular matter. No quarter was given by either side, nor expected. Yet it was not a physical battle; no lives were lost, though careers were ruined. The 1897 ascendance of a new Redemptorist Superior General, Fr. Matthias Raus, who was friendly to Rampolla, gave the Americanists a chance to remove a noteworthy member of the other side.

The same year as his accession, Raus wrote Mueller the following letter:

> Reverend Father,
> I have heard from Most Reverend Father Visitor that you can be influenced neither by him nor by Father Provincial to refrain from publishing your writings, in which you still defend the thesis which you have been ordered again and again no longer to defend. Truly I must confess that I did not think you were so stubborn of mind and spirit as to esteem lightly the commands of your Superiors, so many times repeated. And that especially after (as has been indicated to you) the Sacred Congregation of the Holy Office itself has given you the same prohibition.
>
> [It is interesting to note that no document from the Holy Office regarding Mueller's case apparently had ever been published. Your author suspects that none such existed—a fact of which Mueller would have been aware; notice also that he is not told his thesis is false—just that he may not defend it! Ah, the wonders of double-think].
>
> And so I command you, in virtue of holy obedience, which you have promised to show forth, having openly professed your vows among us, not to spread any writings among the people or to do anything whatsoever in public; and know that, if you do otherwise (which God forbid) you will sin most gravely, and will deserve to be expelled from the Congregation. (*From the Housetops*, Serial no. 31, 1988, pp. 61-62).

Here we see no indication of the intrinsic value (or lack thereof) of Mueller's views: simply "obey or else," which has often been used in unpleasant ways in recent times to prevent religious from upholding Catholic truth. But, in the words of one priest, "Faith is greater than obedience."

This was not a choice Fr. Mueller was forced to make. By the time Raus' letter arrived, he was already in failing health. He lived long enough to see the issuance on 22 January 1899 of Leo XIII's encyclical *Testem Benevolentiae* against the Americanists with whom Mueller had struggled for so many years; of course, there was no attempt to back up the Papal condemnation with actions, nor even to reward those whose faithful and painful combats were at long last upheld by Rome. Mueller lasted a few months longer, enjoying his Golden Jubilee at Annapolis, and dying on 28 August 1899, the Feast of St. Augustine. His principles were vindicated; the Americanists had not triumphed.

But he was not alone among proponents of the traditional teaching. His great contemporary, Fr. Arnold Damen, S.J., (1815-1890) was a native of the Netherlands. He was one of the Jesuit novices brought to this country by Fr. De Smet. Responsible for the founding of most of the great Catholic institutions of Chicago, including Loyola University, he was, moreover, renowned as a preacher, conducting parish missions and lecturing on the faith to open meetings in virtually every major city of the United States. At one time he was said to be better known and more influential than any other priest or bishop in the country. Doubtless it was this fame and influence which preserved him from the treatment meted out to Fr. Mueller.

He needed such preservation, for the things he preached aloud to Protestant audiences were quite as challenging as anything Fr. Mueller wrote:

> ...what kind of faith must a man have to be saved? Will any faith do? Why, if any faith will do, the devil himself will be saved, for the Bible says the devils believe and tremble. It is not, therefore, a matter of indifference what religion a man professes; he must profess the right and true religion, and without that there is no hope of salvation, for it stands to reason, my dear people, that if God reveals a thing or teaches a thing, He wants to be believed. Not to believe is to insult God. Doubting His word, or even believing with doubt and hesitating, is an insult to God,

because it is doubting His Sacred Word. We must, therefore, believe without doubting, without hesitating.

I have said, out of the Catholic Church there is no divine faith—can be no divine faith outside of that Church. Some of my Protestant friends will be shocked at this, to hear me say that out of the Catholic Church there is no divine faith, and that without faith there is no salvation, but damnation. (sermon, *The One True Church,* impr. Michael Corrigan, Archbishop of New York).

Such was the tenor of all his preaching, and from it he made many converts. As written of him shortly after his death on 1 January 1890, "He cared nothing for applause or criticism. He was working to save souls." Both the circumstances of his work and the relatively early time of his death (with the influence noted earlier) effectively insulated him from Americanist fury.

But by the time Damen died, the Americanists had already scored a victory which, unnoticed by their opponents, guaranteed them eventual control of the American Church. This was the insertion by Cardinal Gibbons into the *Baltimore Catechism* of certain questions regarding baptism in 1884. The child was asked how many kinds of Baptism there are, and was expected to reply that there are three: of water, of blood, and of desire. Thus, speculation was erected into dogma. Generations of American Catholics were raised supposing that these ideas were as much a part of the Faith as the Trinity. In later additions, the traditional metaphor of the Church as the Ark of Salvation was amended to speak of "virtuous" non-Catholics as being in little boats attached to that Ark by thin (and presumably) less sure ropes. Doubtless Noah would have been surprised to see them! But in any case, by this means the traditional teaching of the Church was made to seem quite alien to most of those raised with this catechism. After the collapse of catechetics in the wake of Vatican II, the comparative orthodoxy of the *Baltimore Catechism* seemed so much better than what was being taught in Catholic Schools, that every word of it was given by many faithful Catholics practically the status of Holy Writ. The idea that it could have been adulterated by earlier (and so more restrained) heterodoxy became unthinkable. But such was the case. Both the *Irish Catechism* and the famed *Penny Catechism* retain the traditional teaching encompassed within those of St. John Neumann and Fr. DeHarbe.

So then, what was the situation in the first years of the new century? The liberal teaching on salvation became a major plank of the Modernists, who watered it down ever further; yet even many of their opponents, wrongly assuming it to have the authority of both Trent and St. Thomas (and of course, with every assertion on the part of "reputable" theologians that this was the case, the idea gathered ever more weight) held more limited versions of the same concept. Limited, yet just as dangerous, for the difference was one of degree rather than kind, and over time its "conservative" adherents must follow their more adventurous confreres as the whole tenor of the question turned steadily leftward.

In Rome, the same process infiltrated the Roman Seminaries and the functionaries of the Curia, the latter of whom had a great degree of control over whose teachings were condemned, and whose not. Similarly, in Europe and America, Catholic facilities of higher learning and the more advanced religious orders absorbed the new teaching, spreading it among all who passed through their gates. A further foothold was given it wherever the *Baltimore Catechism* was used. Pope Benedict XV might write a few years later in *Ad beatissimi* (*Papal Teachings: The Church*, 761) that,

> The nature of the Catholic faith is such that nothing can be added, nothing taken away. Either it is held in its entirety or it is rejected totally. This is the Catholic faith which, unless a man believes faithfully and firmly, he cannot be saved.

But neither that Pope nor his saintly predecessor could do much more than retard these errors slithering on.

Who held to the traditional teaching, then, besides those Popes? Firstly, it was held firmly in the cloister, particularly among contemplatives, who spent their lives in contemplation of the Divine Presence. So Dom Columba Marmion, O.S.B., (1858-1923) abbot of Maredsous and generally acknowledged a master of the spiritual life, after describing the necessity of faith for justification, writes:

> But faith is not enough.
> When Our Lord sent forth His Apostles to continue His sanctifying mission upon earth, He said: "he that believeth not shall be condemned" (Mark 16:16). He adds nothing further as for those who will not believe because, faith being the root of all justification, everything done without faith is valueless in God's

sight: ["Without faith it is impossible to please God" (Hebrews, 11:15), but for those who believe, Christ adds the reception of Baptism as the condition of incorporation into His kingdom. "He that believeth and is baptized, shall be saved" (Mark 16:16). St. Paul likewise says that "as many of you as have been baptized... have put on Christ" (Gal, 33:27). Baptism is the first in date of all the Sacraments; Divine life is first infused into us at Baptism. (*Christ The Life of The Soul*, p. 151)

Yet even the great Don Marmion received a bit of persecution for his stand in this and other matters. He feuded with his local ordinary, the liberal Cardinal Mercier (who has nevertheless a great reputation for holiness). Apparently, the latter among other things, compelled Marmion to include grudging references to "desire" in his published works; these can be seen in those published during Marmion's lifetime inevitably preceded by a dash or relegated to footnotes. Not at all in keeping with the style of his work, they only enter the body of it in Marmion's posthumous publications. In any case, Mercier did not attend his funeral.

So similarly, Dom Prosper Gueranger, O.S.B. (1805-1875) abbot of Solesmes, reviver both of Benedictine life in France and of Gregorian Chant, and primary author of the monumental *Liturgical Year*, was a believer in the traditional teaching of the Church: "This society is the Spouse of Christ; it is by her that he produces his elect. She is the one only Mother of the elect; out of her bosom there is no salvation" (*op. cit.,* vol. VIII, bk. II., pp. 130-131). Like the works of his confrere of Maredsous, Dom Gueranger's occasionally feature a fleeting reference to desire; like them also, these are obviously added on, the supplemental work of other, lesser hands.

Apart from Mystics like these, Ultra-Realists by virtue of their absorption of the ambience of the Church's devotions and liturgy, Missionaries also tended to retain the traditional position. Constantly working to save souls, these brave men and women spent their lives solely on the basis of there being no salvation outside of the Church. If this was so for domestic missionaries such as Frs. Damen and Mueller, how much truer was it for those who ventured out to heathen lands in the wake of St. Francis Xavier? Each of their converts repeated to them a "Profession of Faith" which included the phrase: "...knowing that no one can be saved without that faith which the Holy Catholic Apostolic Roman Church holds, believes, and teaches..."

In America, the floods of non-English-speaking Catholic immigrants (Germans, Dutch, Czechs, Poles, French-Canadians, Latin Americans, Slovakians, Croats, Slovenes, Lithuanians, Portuguese, Belgians, Hungarians, Austrians, and the various Eastern Rites) rarely used the *Baltimore Catechism* in instructing their children. Their priests in turn taught the same Faith they themselves had learned in their countries of origin. This pattern tended to continue for as long as these groups evaded assimilation. A French-Canadian friend, for instance, attended a national parish elementary school in 1930s New England, and there was taught by the nuns that no one could be saved outside the Church. When he began taking English-language doctrine classes at the High School level, he was introduced to desire and invincible ignorance and all the other slithering.

Mystics, Missionaries, and simple Immigrants: these tended to be the holders of the traditional teaching of No Salvation Outside the Church in the first few decades of the 20th Century. Interestingly enough, no one held this doctrine more strongly than St. Frances Xavier Cabrini (1850-1917), who was all three. Foundress of the Missionary Sisters of the Sacred Heart, and of 67 hospitals, orphanages, schools and convents, she was also a wonder-working mystic, whose miracles caused many to consider her a saint even before she died. (One is reminded of a character in a play, an actress who claimed she knew all about religion, having "once played Mother Cabrini"!). Mother Cabrini was dispatched by Leo XIII from her native Italy to work among her countrymen in the U.S., becoming a citizen in 1909. Her comments on this matter are worth noting:

> Many Protestants have almost the same practices as we, only they do not see their way to submit to the Holy Father and attach themselves to the true Ark of Salvation... They do not want to become Catholics and unite themselves under the banner of truth wherein alone there is true salvation. (*Travels of F.X. Cabrini*, p. 84).
>
> He who does not enter by the door of the fold shall not have salvation. The door of the fold is the Catholic Church and union with the Head who represents Jesus. (op. cit., p. 170)
>
> Of what avail is it, children, if Protestants lead naturally pure, honest lives, yet possess virtues which lack the interior impulse of the Holy Ghost? They may well say: "We do no harm; we lead

good lives"; but, if they do not enter the true fold of Christ, all their protestations are in vain, because a really good life is that which is so formed and ordered as to lead to the Way that is Blessed and Eternal. Without this admirable order and relationship, a good life is of no value. These poor people do not enter the door of the true fold of Christ because they do not know Christ perfectly, or at least do not follow His commands in their entirety. (op. cit., p. 171).

It is interesting also that of our four American citizen Saints—three immigrants (Mother Cabrini and Ss. John Neumann and Rose Phillipine Duschesne) and one convert (St. Elizabeth Ann Seton)—all were strong adherents of No Salvation Outside the Church. Interesting too is it that as of this writing (2017) we have produced only a single native-born American cradle-Catholic saint, although Canada and Latin America have produced a number. Oh well, what we may lack in sanctity we surely make up for in funds.

Indeed we do. For 1917 saw not only Mother Cabrini's death, but the U.S.'s entry into World War I. To coordinate Catholic participation in the effort, the American Bishops formed the National Catholic War Council. After the War, this was renamed the National Catholic Welfare Conference, which was in turn succeeded in 1968 by the United States Catholic Conference and the National Conference of Catholic Bishops. From the beginning, these successive bodies worked to impose upon the Church in the States first Americanism and then Modernism, uniting the heterodox bishops against their orthodox brethren, and the whole against Rome. In this fateful year also, Russia fell to Communist Revolution, and Our Lady appeared at Fatima. Quite a year, 1917.

The next year saw the end of the War, and the fall of Austria-Hungary, last remnant of the Holy Roman Empire and premier Catholic power, at the behest of American president Woodrow Wilson. Europe was devastated economically, America was the dominant nation, and a new order of things began to be established. A decade later, Cardinal Mundelein of Chicago arranged a loan to save the Holy See from bankruptcy. Within a year, the Lateran Treaty was signed and its financial settlement relieved the Vatican from total monetary dependence on the American Church—for the moment. In the meantime, the focus of anti-traditional theology swung back to Europe.

ATTACK ON THE DOGMA INCREASES

Modernism had slowly grown, its ground prepared by the sort of rationalistic neo-Thomism condemned by Maritain at the end of his life. This was a sort of convoluted philosophizing which, while it proceeded logically from point to point, made little sense in its totality. It was given further impulse to denude the traditional teachings of the Church on salvation by the camaraderie forged with non-Catholics on both sides during the 1914-1918 War. This denuding was characterized by the facility with which the words themselves: "No Salvation Outside the Church," could be artfully dodged or slithered around, allowing the theologian to deny the meaning of the words while claiming to hold them formally.

Most often quoted and best known of these was the French Jesuit Fr. J. Bainvel, whose little book *Is There Salvation Outside the Catholic Church* is a monument to special pleading and double meaning. First appearing in English in that fateful year of 1917, it has rarely been out of print since. Its thesis is intriguing in a sense. He maintains that yes, there is no Salvation outside the Church, but Invincible Ignorance excuses one from belonging to it. It is he who mistranslated the local encyclical of Pius IV which your author noted earlier. This mistranslation was needed if that Pontiff was to be made to endorse Bainvel's position—though of course Pius did not. While Bainvel admits that there was no such teaching earlier, he claims that it has come about in stages. But this is not dogma; what kind of a statement is it that is absolute with one breath, and then near completely voided (for most men are not Catholics) in the next? What would have been the point of saying No Salvation Outside the Church in the first place? Bainvel sums up his teaching (*op. cit.,* p. 54) in these words:

> Souls affiliated with the Church *unconsciously* are united to her by invisible ties, for they are affiliated with her internally, by

an *implicit desire*, which God is pleased to regard as equivalent to external membership.

Ah, but the slithering is all about us now! Church membership creeps up on one unawares, dragging him into Heaven willy-nilly! Why send out Missionaries? Why baptize with water at all? Why pay priests to write? Are you all aghast?

The German priest Karl Adam (1876-1966), attempted a theory which at least had a bit more coherence: that Catholics *per se* belong to the "body" of the Church, while "good" non-Catholics are part of the "soul" of the Church, whatever that might be. This thesis he advanced in his 1924 opus, *The Spirit of Catholicism*. While this idea became very popular among many clerics, Pius XII laid it to rest in his 1943 Encyclical *Mystici corporis*. Not only did he say therein that "Actually only those are to be numbered among the members of the Church who have received the laver of regeneration and profess the true faith" (Denzinger 2286), but he declared the Holy Ghost to be the "Soul of the Church." This path of getting non-Catholics somehow into the Church was cut off.

But where there is a will, there is a way to slither. Fr. Henri de Lubac, S.J. attempted also to square the circle in his 1938 book *Catholicism* (p. 125):

> As "unbelievers" are, in the design of providence, indispensable for building the Body of Christ, they must in their own way profit from their vital connection with this same Body. By an extension of the dogma of the communion of saints, it seems right to think that though they themselves are not in the normal way of salvation, they will be able nevertheless to obtain this salvation by virtue of the mysterious bonds which unite them to the faithful. In short, they can be saved because they are an integral part of that humanity which is to be saved.

Ah, well, here we go again. "An extension of... the communion of saints;" "it seems right to think...." "mysterious bonds..." Slither, slither, slither, eh, Fr. De Lubac? Here we see the tendencies of Fr. Bainvel brought along further. If all this is so, then why bother with the Church? Leave it all to that "mysterious" realm whence come all these bonds, leave God to perform His saving work in secret, and leave honest folk out of it... and of course, richer by whatever they would have given the Church.

But the end is not yet. Perhaps the crowning moment of this kind of gibberish was touched by Maritain, in his unrepentant younger days as oracle of Neo-Thomism. Commenting upon the Bull *Cantate domino* of the Council of Florence, which, as we saw, outlined the four sorts of folk who cannot go to heaven: heretics, schismatics, Jews, and pagans, he says:

> What matters here is the declaration itself, not the manner in which one understands it in that epoch... according to the mentality of the epoch, without having been conscious of the ambiguity... It is with time that the ambiguity in question appeared—and at the same stroke the true sense in which the declaration must be taken. There has therefore been a mutation, not with regard to the declaration itself, but with regard to the manner in which those who formulated it understood it. The declaration is infallibly true (provided it is rightly understood).

Oh no! *Et tu, Jacques?* Ambiguity? Please, dear and gentle readers, let us reread the definition of Florence here cited.

> The most Holy Roman Church believes, professes, and teaches that none of those who are not within the Catholic Church, not only pagans, but also Jews and heretics and schismatics, can have a share in eternal life, but that they will go into the everlasting fire prepared for the devil and his angels, unless before death they shall have entered into that Church; and that so important is the unity of this ecclesiastical body that only those abiding within this unity can profit from the sacraments of the Church unto salvation, and that they alone can receive an eternal reward for their fasts, their almsgiving, their other works of Christian piety and duties of a Christian soldier. No one, let his alms-giving be as great as it may, no one, even if he pour out his blood for the name of Christ, can be saved unless he abide within the bosom and unity of the Catholic Church. *(Denzinger 714).*

You may not agree with it, you may think it mean-spirited and nasty, you may think whatsoever you please about it. But you will understand that regardless of opinions, your author can find no trace of ambiguity therein! Quite the contrary, which is what makes so many folk uncomfortable about it. But I will leave critique of this passage of Maritain to the illustrious Dr. John Senior:

> Surely no Protestant in his right mind will accept an argument like this as the price of peace, because the whole Christian revelation, church authority, all authority, the noble mind of Maritain, and reason itself are here overthrown. "Words," said [Humpty-Dumpty] to Alice, "mean exactly whatever I say they mean." Go back to start! Begin again. We are here at the first of first principles. A definition that includes its contradictory is not a definition at all... "The definition is true (provided it is rightly understood)." That is either a truism—anything must be rightly understood—or what used to be called "jesuitical." Understood by whom? Gospels, Epistles, the Law and the Prophets, creeds, confessions—all these are infallibly true if "rightly understood" according to the ideals of the French Revolution and the mind of Maritain, and the mind of the mind that understands the mind of Maritain... *Infallible?* Such music hath a dying fall. (*The Death of Christian Culture*, p. 5).

Obviously, Senior's criticism of Maritain is equally applicable to De Lubac, Adam, Bainvel, the Paulists, and so on. Obviously also, holders of such views would like to be able to say simply that non-Catholics can be saved as non-Catholics; this would have an admirable logic and simplicity. But it would also require such theologians to deny explicitly a revealed doctrine. Faced with this dilemma, when they cannot stand up in the light of day with their actual belief, they must slither.

Despite the obvious absurdity and even self-contradiction of their varying explanations, these ideas slithered right into seminary curriculums all over inter-war Europe—even ones which were otherwise orthodox. The products of these places in later years clung to whatever they had been taught with all their might in the face of an ever triumphant and resurgent Modernism. If it came to them from their seminaries, it must be so. Were they not pre-Vatican II? Were these things not taught to them by the teachers whom they revered and whose orthodoxy was unimpeachable? One victim of this syndrome was Archbishop Marcel Lefebvre. In his book *An Open Letter to Concerned Catholics* (pp. 80-81), after explaining eloquently that present day Ecumenism runs counter to the doctrine "No Salvation Outside the Church," His Grace goes on to observe:

> Does this mean that no Protestant, no Muslim, no Buddhist or animist will be saved? No, it would be a second error to think that. Those who cry for intolerance in interpreting St. Cyprian's

formula *Outside the Church there is no salvation*, also reject the Creed, "I accept one baptism for the remission of sins," and are insufficiently instructed as to what baptism is. There are three ways of receiving it: the baptism of water; the baptism of blood (that of the martyrs who confessed their faith while still catechumens); and baptism of desire. Baptism of desire can be *explicit*. Many times in Africa I heard one of our catechumens say to me, "Father, baptize me straightaway because if I die before you come again, I shall go to hell." I told him, "No, if you have no mortal sin on your conscience and if you desire baptism, then you already have the grace in you."

The doctrine of the Church also recognizes *implicit* baptism of desire. This consists of doing the will of God. God knows all men and he knows that amongst Protestants, Muslims, Buddhists, and in the whole of humanity there are men of good will. They receive the grace of baptism without knowing it, but in an effective way. In this way they become part of the Church.

Well, well. We are back again at Fr. Bainvel's poor conscripts of grace, unable to avoid Church membership even if they tried. In truth, I fear that the catechumens to whom Mgr. Lefebvre refers had a better grasp of the logic of their situation in the light of revelation than did their missionary; if they already had the grace in them, why have the missionary return, and possibly block their way to heaven by obligating to obey the rules of the Church and risk Hell? Your author is also a bit uncomprehending; how does insisting that there is only one baptism contradict the Creed's statement that there is one baptism? Lastly, the good Archbishop tosses in a red herring with his reference to those who "cry for intolerance" vis-à-vis St. Cyprian's doctrine. It is not intolerant at all to insist that words mean what they say. The statement of St. Cyprian (and of all those Fathers, Doctors, Popes, and Councils who so solemnly echoed him) may be called erroneous by Lefebvre; it matters not that the whole of the Church's credibility rises or falls with it, it might indeed be called erroneous. Or it may be that St. Cyprian and his sundry echoers were all incoherent, and quite incapable of attaching any real meaning to the words in this phrase. But in such cases your author would not call them intolerant; merely wrong, mad, or wicked (if the former two qualities were not unintentional and they simply wanted to mislead the faithful). Contrariwise, it would seem highly inappropriate to call those who insist that the words be taken at their face value "intolerant." "Tolerance" does not seem to be an issue here—only truth.

That such ideas could gain acceptance despite their novelty—even on the part of such an astute observer as Mgr. Lefebvre—only shows that they were held by enough clerics in high places to appear to endue them with a specious "authority" all their own. With such clerics in charge of the day-to-day running of the Church, both in Rome and in many dioceses and religious orders, it would be expected that signs of the change in belief would show at last in the Church's prayer life. After all, *lex orandi, lex credendi*, "the law of prayer is the law of belief." Sure enough, a comparison of two editions of the *Raccolta*, the manual of indulgenced prayers, compiled in Latin in 1928 and 1950 respectively, and each printed in English two years later, is quite revealing.

The decree preceding the foreword of the 1952 edition, signed by Nicholas Cardinal Canali, Major Penitentiary, says that his "Office deemed it advisable to review the entire work carefully, to delete certain portions which appeared to be somewhat unsatisfactory…" What prayers were "unsatisfactory" in the pontificate of Pius XII, that were permissible in that of Pius XI? What was the criterion employed? We are not told, and so we must look for ourselves. To begin with, the 1930 edition includes prayers for the conversion of Scandinavia, the Greek Schismatics, the Muslims, England, Japan, the Jews, Heathens, the Chinese and Mongols, Freemasons, Africa, and the Welsh. These are all gone from the 1952 version. One can see why. No. 377, the *Prayer to Our Lady of Africa for the Conversion of the Mussulmans and other Infidels*, indulgenced for 300 Days by Leo XII in 1896, contains the chilling words:

> Do not allow, O Mother of mercy, that these unhappy people, who are, like us, thy children, should continue to fall into hell, despite the merits of JESUS CHRIST and the most cruel death he suffered for their salvation.

Further on, the prayer asks Our Lady to send missionaries… "to rescue them from death and Satan…"

No. 306, similarly indulgenced by Leo XIII, is a *Prayer for Reunion*. It tells us that "it is impossible to obtain salvation except in union with the successor of St. Peter." Nor is no. 622, the *Prayer for the Conversion of Freemasons*, with its warning about souls "most miserably deceived by the treacherous snares of Freemasons, and going more and more astray in the way of perdition," likely to become popular in these United States, where the Masonic Order is practically the established religion.

This is not to say that the 1952 edition does not still retain many wonderful prayers, nor that others were not added thereunto that have made the 1930 version even better. One prayer (no. 626) even says that "the Holy Catholic Church is the one true Church, outside of which neither holiness nor salvation can be found." But it is surely undeniable that the actively Missionary stance of the older collection has been greatly tamed; instead of wanting to convert all the World to Catholicism, which is the tone of the prior edition's prayers, 1952 simply wants Catholics to have a strong devotional life. Doubtless this last is much better than a good deal of what passes for piety today; but it is still a decline and a change in direction.

Yet it is understandable. For in the interim, World War II had broken out, and like the preceding war brought many Catholics and non-Catholics into close contact and mutual endeavor. This had the natural effect of causing many of the former to want the latter saved "just the way they are." It also had once again the result of impoverishing the European Church and throwing the Vatican into the hands of the American Church with its secure finances; and Pius XII felt it necessary to cooperate closely with the States, "Leader of the Free World," against the specter of Communism. These developments, combined with the continued doctrinal decay we have been chronicling, bore some mighty strange fruit, around which errors slithered.

Perhaps the clearest indication of the way things were going was that some American priests, after the War ended, began on their own to drop from St. Francis Xavier's prayer which we saw earlier the words "Remember, Lord, how to thy dishonor hell is being filled with these souls" at the prayer's public recitation during the Novena of Grace. In 1948, the new French order called the Fathers of Cherbourg was ordered to stop preaching "No Salvation Outside the Church" at their retreats by the local ordinary. The Fathers refused, and the bishop took no overt action. But bit by bit the fledgling institute was asked to provide retreats for ever fewer groups, and missions for ever fewer parishes.

This was typical of the way that, all around the world, holders of the traditional Church teaching on this topic were slowly (or not so slowly) squeezed out. This process would doubtless have continued quietly, had it not been for one priest and one incident: Fr. Leonard Feeney and the Boston Heresy Case. These would at once give the liberals a buzz-word to call the Church's teaching (and so dismiss it) and to establish an important precedent in misuse of Canon Law.

Fr. Feeney wrote a poem which admirably summed up the doctrinal situation in the Church just prior to the Second World War:

> The cycle has swung to sorrow,
> Our ranks have begun to fail;
> We know not what gate of Hell
> Tomorrow will not prevail.
>
> The foam-at-the-mouth is frothing
> In the Beast with the flashing tooth;
> The Hound that was sent on the scent of Nothing,
> Has found the Truth.

Of this priest and that case, as well as developments involving Karl Rahner, Vatican II, and the present Holy Father, we shall treat in the next chapters.

VEILED SIGN OF CONTINUITIES

It should be born in mind that, while the doctrinal decay we have been discussing was great, it had not, by the late 1940s, done much outward damage. However rotten much of seminary and Catholic high education might be, however rife heresy might be among the more influential clergy, there was little outward sign of it visible to the casual observer. It was a situation reminiscent of a termite infested chair; it looks completely solid until you sit upon it, whereupon it dissolves into dust—leaving you in a confused heap.

Indeed, in the year of Grace 1947 the Church appeared to be flourishing. Through the 1920s, 30s, and 40s, Catholic lay apostolates mushroomed and converts flocked into the Church. In Great Britain, a host of Catholic writers appeared, addressing a vast variety of social, political, literary, and religious topics: G.K. Chesterton, Hilaire Belloc, Eric Gill, Christopher Hollis, E.I. Watkin, Sir Shane Leslie, Sir Compton Mackenzie, Caryl Houselander, Vincent McNabb, O.P., The Meynells, Christopher Dawson, Alfred Noyes, Douglas Jerrold, Roy Campbell, J.R.R. Tolkien, Evelyn Waugh, C.C. Martindale, Arnold Lunn, Montague Summers, and Grahame Greene, to name a very few. Across the Channel, France boasted such names as Georges Bernanos, Francois Mauriac, Paul Claudel, and Henri Gheon. Indeed, every country in Catholic Europe had similar boasts.

In the rest of the English-speaking world, parallel efforts were underway. Canada was host to the Antigonish movement among the Nova Scotia fishing parishes, and Fr. Lionel Groulx was active in Quebec with his *Action Nationale*. Australia had the Campion Society, The Australian *Catholic Worker*, and the Catholic Social Movement. On the American scene were: Dorothy Day and Peter Maurin who founded the *Catholic Worker*, Baroness De Hueck the inter-racial Friendship House, and the controversial Fr. Charles E. Couglin the National Union for Social Justice. Acting as a link between the various Anglophone Catholic movements were Maisie

Ward (from a prominent Catholic English family), and Frank Sheed, an Australian-born convert. Both deeply committed to the Apostolate, they formed after their marriage a publishing house, Sheed and Ward, to make Catholic writers available to readers all over the British Empire and the United States.

One of the most prominent stars on the Catholic lecture circuit in the U.S. during the 1930s was the Jesuit Fr. Leonard Feeney, literary editor of the Jesuit magazine *America*. An accomplished poet, his books were a fixture in every Catholic institution during the late 30s and early 40s. His abilities as a raconteur and mimic were proverbial: among his specialties in imitation were doing Katherine Hepburn describing Joe Lewis at a boxing match; Franklin Roosevelt speaking on Mother Cabrini and sanctifying grace; and Archbishop Fulton Sheen commenting on Coca Cola. Perhaps typical of his sense of humor was an incident in 1935. Walking down 5th Avenue in New York between Frank Sheed and Maisie Ward, he suddenly grabbed each of their arms, exclaiming "I'm the 'and' in Sheed and Ward!"

But there was another and more serious side to Leonard Feeney. Entering the Jesuits in 1914 at the age of 17, he had thrown himself into his theological studies. In those days, the Jesuits gave their younger members one of two theological courses: the Short Course and the Long Course. The former basically comprised the same sort of teaching given ordinary diocesan priests, sufficient to guide them through their parish work. The Long Course was given to the brightest, and was much more in-depth. It provided a systematic exposition of every detail of Catholic theology, including disputed points. There it was that Feeney acquired his life-long and intensely personal love of the Fathers and Doctors of the Church. But it was also there that he encountered adherents of the slithering errors we discussed in the last chapter. While he received in the end the highest grades in the Long Course than any American Jesuit had ever rated up to that time, he refused an invitation to finish his studies at the Gregorian in Rome. His stomach was ulcerated, and he had already acquired a visceral hatred of error; two years of the New Theology there would surely kill him. So he was sent to Oxford University to study literature instead, fell in with various members of the English Catholic Literary Revival, and prepared for an apostolate in letters, eventually rising to his *America* post.

However inopportune Pius XI's strategy of gutting Catholic parties in favor of Catholic Action was in Continental Europe, the Pontiff's encouragement of Catholic Action in English speaking countries was very wise. In those places, Catholics had no political parties anyway, and little influence at the onset of Pius XI's pontificate. But in line with the Pope's prescription for Catholic Action, various Catholic guilds, sodalities, societies, clubs, and apostolates multiplied as we have seen. They were intended for all the manifold activities Catholics engaged in, and so in America ranged from the National Catholic Rural Life Conference for farms, to the Auto League of the Sacred Heart for motorists. Prominent among these bodies were the various Catholic Student movements, such as the New Clubs. On 19 March 1940, a center for Catholic students at Harvard and Radcliffe was established in Cambridge's Harvard Square by Mrs. Catherine Goddard Clarke and several converts, including the now-famous theologian Fr. Avery Dulles, S.J.

St. Benedict Center, as the new organization was called, provided both social events and lectures for the students. Shortly after the Center opened, Fr. Feeney was brought down from Weston College where he was teaching, to speak. His easy manner and ability to explain difficult religious problems in a simple yet logical manner soon made him a general favorite. Eventually, the students asked him to speak every Thursday evening on various Catholic topics. He did, and these sessions were soon packed. Eventually, Feeney became Spiritual Director of the Center in 1942; there then followed five years—years of War and Reconstruction for the rest of the world, and quiet and steady growth for the Center.

Harvard College was founded in 1636 as a breeding ground for Congregationalist ministers. After turning Unitarian in the early 19th Century, it soon became entirely rationalist; for all that it retains a Divinity School and a Memorial Chapel. Therein the most un- and anti-Christian philosophies were taught; the fact that much of America's ruling elite were trained there boded ill for the country. When Catholics acquired the money and prestige necessary to send their children there they did so, with the result that many of these lost their faith. Of the non-Catholics, a good number lost whatever beliefs they had had, and became total agnostics or atheists.

To combat these trends, Fr. Feeney guided his charges into an ever more intensive study of the Scriptures (in Latin and Greek),

Fathers, Doctors, Popes, and Councils. This return to the sources fired them with zeal for the Faith, but it also resulted in many converts from the non-Catholic Harvard-Radcliffe studentry. At last, in 1946, this zeal bubbled over into a student magazine, *From The Housetops*. This title implied the strait-forward manner in which they wished to broadcast Catholicism.

At first, all seemed well. Archbishop Cushing of Boston himself contributed two articles to it, as did several prominent Catholic writers from around the country, as well as the students themselves of course. But the students, under Fr. Feeney's tutelage, began to notice that American Catholicism was not so much Catholic as American; and that American was not so much non- as anti-Catholic. This was increasingly reflected in their writings. At last there was printed an article in the September 1947 issue entitled "Sentimental Theology," by a Lebanese professor at Boston College named Fakhri Maluf.

This piece was a pillorying, not of sentiment, but, in its author's words, "of sentimentality." In it, Dr. Maluf argued for an end to all expression connoting exceptions to the necessity of the Church for salvation, reiterating traditional teaching and answering the usual objections thereto. He concluded by writing:

> But wouldn't our profession of faith in such uncompromising terms make non-Catholics unhappy? Would it not disturb them to know that we think they are not on the way to heaven? Well, it could disturb them only the moment they begin to believe the Christian story, and then they need not remain worried. The Catholic Church does not proclaim the exclusive salvation of one race or class of people, but invites every man to the great joy of being united with Christ in the communion of saints. The Catholic truth is not a sad story for which we need to apologize; it is a proclamation of the greatest good news that could ever be told. No matter how sternly its message is phrased, it is still the one and only hope in the world. Only love and security can afford to be severe. When we say that outside the Church there is no salvation, we are also and at the same time announcing that inside the Church there is salvation. The world already knows the sad part of our story, because the world finds no salvation in the world. The Church does not have to tell the unbelievers that they are in sin and despair; they know that in the depth of their hearts. What is new to the world in the Christian story is that, through Mary, the gates of heaven are opened and that we are invited to become

brothers of Jesus in the Eternal Kingdom of God. This is not a story which can be told with the subdued and hesitant voice of sentimental theology.

After this kind of challenge, the storm clouds began to gather.

Converts continued to be made from Harvard, and many of these began to resign from that college. Of these, one of the most prominent was Temple Morgan, kinsman of J.P. Now it ought to be understood that the Brahmins, the Boston subsection of the WASPs (White Anglo-Saxon Protestants) were no friends of the Faith. They occupied many of the region's and the nation's most prestigious political posts and social positions. These did not send their sons to Harvard to have them become Catholics and to resign from the college! It was inevitable that trouble would arise.

In mid-1948, Archbishop Cushing was a guest for dinner at High Table in Harvard's Lowell House. There the college's concerns over its losses were brought up to the prelate's attention. At this point, it should be made clear that among the Irish in the diaspora there is often an odd sort of obsequiousness toward the Ascendancy, the Protestant establishment in whichever English-speaking land they find themselves. In America, being mixed with Americanism, it can be frightful indeed. So it was that, on 8 August, 1948, Cushing gave a speech at a seminary in Milton, Massachusetts:

> I cannot understand any Catholic who has any prejudice whatsoever against a Jew or other non-Catholic. If there is any Catholic organization harboring such prejudices I will assume the responsibility of remedying it. A Catholic cannot harbor animosity against men, women and children of another creed, nationality or color.

It was apparent to those involved, both at the Center and at Harvard, which institution was being spoken of. (In due course the Archbishop would receive his Honorary (!) Degree from a grateful Harvard.) It is interesting to note that the Archbishop's use of terms like "animosity" and "prejudice" in this regard. An odd set of folk, the Centerites must have been, whose animosity and prejudice toward others was shown by their trying to get those others to join the Church they belonged to! Calling upon both Cushing and John Wright, the latter's auxiliary, students from the Center were assured that no action would be taken against the Center without a hearing. About a week later, both prelates boarded ship for Rome, to make a pilgrimage to the tomb of Pope St. Pius X.

On 25 August, Fr. Feeney received a letter from Fr. J.J. McEleney, Jesuit provincial for Boston, telling him that he was to be transferred to Holy Cross College in Worcester. But the Center students asked him to enquire as to the reason for his transfer. Fr. Feeney called the Provincial, who agreed to meet him. Here is that conversation, important because of what it reveals about the tactics of the authorities in the case:

> Fr. Feeney said: "What is the point of my being changed, Father?"
> The Provincial replied: "Higher Authorities."
> "What higher authorities?"
> "We can't go into that."
> "You mean by higher authorities the Archbishop or the Bishop?"
> "I'm not saying it was anyone. You are being changed, dear Father, for the good of the Province."
> "But I don't work just for the good of the Province. I work for the greater glory of God. I was down in the status for the year as assigned to St. Benedict Center." *["Status" is the name given by the Jesuits to the publications of assignments for the following year, for all the members of the Society. Status occurs at the very beginning of the Summer, never later than 31 July.]*
> "You have already written to Monsignor Hickey?" [Hickey was Vicar General of the Archdiocese, and so in charge during Cushing's and Wright's absence.]
> "Yes."
> "Don't you think it would have been decent of you, Father, to have called me in and discussed it with me first, before you wrote to Monsignor?"
> "Maybe I should have."
> "It isn't too late to change now."
> "I'm afraid it is."
> "Well, can't you revoke the decision?"
> "No, Father, I'm not in a position to do that."
> "Well, would you, if you could?"
> "No, I don't think I would."
> "But, Father, you have never heard my side of the story on St. Benedict Center, and I thought that because you were leaving

me alone and trusting me that what I was doing was agreeable to you. What is being objected to in what I am doing?"

"Your doctrine."

"My doctrine on what?"

"I'm sorry, we can't go into that."

"Won't you tell me what it was so that I can defend myself?"

"I'm sorry, Father, the letter has already gone to the Vicar General, and I'm sure you will respect my wishes and go to Holy Cross on 8 September."

"Father, this is going to be the worst scandal that ever happened if you kick me out this way. The students at St. Benedict Center are committed to me in the school for a whole year. They have given up their homes (many of them come from out of State), and you can't ask this of them. I was appointed in status time. I beg you, in the name of Mary Father, please reconsider it... I'm older than you in the Society, and I am telling you, Father, that the hundreds of boys and girls who have trusted me, and all the children I have in religion, will be scandalized if you throw me out like this without a hearing. They will be confused if you tell them that my doctrine is wrong, without a hearing on that doctrine."

"We have considered all that."

(Catherine G. Clarke, *Loyolas and Cabots*, pp. 101-102).

After this, a flurry of letters and telegrams went out from the students to the voyaging bishops, the Provincial, and various other authorities. Except for one acknowledgement to the first telegram sent Bishop Wright, no reply was ever received. When the 8th arrived, Fr. Feeney packed his bags and made ready to go. The students argued that if he complied, that would be the end of the matter, and the traditional teaching on salvation would sink without a trace. But if he stayed, and forced a hearing or trial on the matter, the doctrine of No Salvation would be reaffirmed—although his reputation might be ruined. Fr. Feeney chose the latter course.

Fr. Feeney and his Provincial exchanged a number of letters in the days immediately following. Fr. Feeney repeated the need for a hearing, if doctrine was the reason for his transfer, the Provincial continued to say that the only issue was Fr. Feeney's refusal to leave the Center. Doctrine or Discipline—that was the nub of the dispute.

There things sat for the moment. But at the Jesuit Boston College, where four men associated with the Center taught, things began to heat up. In a course entitled Modern Science and

Philosophy, Fr. Joseph P. Kelly, S.J., imparted the following statements, recorded in December 1948:

> It is possible for any man to be saved outside the Catholic Church.
> Any man who would say that there is no salvation outside the Church is a heretic.
> If you say there is no salvation outside the Catholic Church, you are a heretic and cannot save your soul.
> The Catholic Church never defined or even suggested that there is no salvation outside it. No Pope, no Council, no Doctor of the Church ever taught that no one can be saved outside the Catholic Church.
> Not only is it possible to be saved outside the Catholic Church, it is even possible to be saved while being an enemy of the Church and actively fighting against it.
> St. Paul was not sinning while persecuting Christ and his Church.
> The dogma that there is no salvation outside the Church applies exclusively to Catholics who have personally left the church. (Clarke, *op. cit.*, 143-144)

This was typical of the sort of thing being taught at the college at that time. In response to this kind of teaching, the four professors sent a letter dated 24 January 1949 to Fr. William Keleher, a president of the college, informing him that,

> ...the following heresies are being taught at Boston College: (1) that there is salvation outside the Church; (2) that any man can be saved without submission to the authority of our Holy Father the Pope.

The same day they received a reply from Keleher, saying that a check with other college officials showed their charges to be groundless, but would they submit a detailed report on the heresies they believed were being taught at the college?

After a conversation in which Keleher insisted that no heresies were prevalent at Boston College, appeals were written to the Holy Father and the General of the Jesuits, charging again that heresy was indeed in the air at Boston College. No real response was received, but the professors were fired anyway.

In all the conversation held between Fr. Feeney with local authorities, it was always the same old thing. Fr. Feeney would ask for a heresy trial, only to be told that he would not get one, and that he was disobedient. Can your author be forgiven for suspecting that no such trial was desirable simply because Fr. Feeney could not be convicted?

At last, the 19 April 1949 issue of the Boston *Pilot*, the Archdiocesan paper, carried a decree by Archbishop Cushing on Fr. Feeney:

> Rev. Leonard Feeney, S.J., because of grave offense against the laws of the Catholic Church has lost the right to perform any priestly function, including preaching and teaching of religion.
>
> Any Catholics who frequent St. Benedict's Center, or who in any way take part in or assist its activities forfeit the right to receive the Sacrament of Penance and Holy Eucharist.
>
> Given at Boston on the 18th day of April 1949
> (Clarke, *op. cit.*, p. 219).

Ah, but what are we to make of this decree? Canon Law requires that the offense be spelled out; a man cannot be punished without specific reason. Was Fr. Feeney a heretic? A murderer? What was the nature of this penalty? Is Fr. Feeney suspended? Silenced? Excommunicated? Interdicted? What of those who "frequented" St. Benedict's Center? Did this apply to those who studied there, ate their lunch there, or to the janitor? Why were not Fr. Feeney and the frequenters given the three warnings required before publication of a penal decree by Canon law? None of these questions can be answered now; but one thing is certain. In Boston, Canon Law had been replaced by Archiepiscopal whim.

At any rate, Fr. Feeney made his own reply at a Press conference the next day:

> The reason I am being silenced is because I believe there is no salvation outside the Catholic Church and without personal submission to our Holy Father, the Pope, and Archbishop Cushing believe there is… and Bishop John Wright believes there is. (Clarke, *op. cit.,* 221).

He ended the conference declaring that he believed all the actions taken against him to be invalid.

Charges and counter-charges flew. What was interesting in particular was that newspaper accounts insisted that disciplinary actions were taken against Fr. Feeney because of his doctrine, while the official communications all dealt with disobedience. Oh, what a kettle of fish!

But this changed on 3 September 1949, when the *Pilot* triumphantly carried the banner headline: HOLY OFFICE CONDEMNS TEACHINGS AND ACTIONS OF ST. BENEDICT'S CENTER. The article went on to explain that a letter from the Holy Office, signed by Cardinal Marchetti-Selvaggiani had been written in response to the actions of Fr. Feeney and the Center students. The letter itself was not printed, only select excerpts, which said among others things that the disturbance was the result of the members of the group's refusal to "revere and obey duly constituted authority." Another quote indicated that while No Salvation Outside the Church is "an incontestable axiom," it must be "understood in the sense in which the Church herself understands it." In a third place, the letter was quoted as urging Center members to "return to Catholic unity."

This Holy Office letter has appeared in various editions of *Denzinger* since 1963, first appearing there under the editorship of Karl Rahner, S.J., at whom we shall gaze more carefully in a moment. But it never appeared in the *Acta Apostolicae Sedis*, the official Latin language registry of all the Holy See's official acts. Indeed, it did not see the light of day at all, until after the death of Marchetti-Selvaggiani a few years later; at that time it was finally published in the *American Ecclesiastical Review*. When Rahner decided to put it into Denzinger, he had to have it translated into Latin from English, whence it was retranslated for the English edition of Denzinger. To say that the authority of such a document is more than a little suspect is perhaps the most charitable thing to be said for it. It has been maintained that the Pope himself carefully went over the wording of the letter; but the only evidence we have of this is that of Cardinal Wright. Given His Eminence's role in this matter, some may not feel called to value his testimony too highly.

On 10 October 1949, Fr. Feeney was dismissed from the Jesuits for the "crime of serious and permanent disobedience…"

Less than a year later, Pius XII issued his encyclical *Humani Generis*, on 21 August 1950. Therein the Pope condemned the teachings of Karl Rahner, Teilhard de Chardin, and their ilk without mentioning their names. As might be expected, this attempt was no more effective than Leo XIII's attack on the Americanists. But some encouragement was given the Center by this document: "Some reduce to an empty formula the necessity of belonging to the True Church in order to attain salvation" (Denzinger 2319). Surely, it was not Fr. Feeney nor was it his young friends who were doing this! It should be noted that, while Fr. Feeney sent a summary of his position to bishops around the world, only three replied favorably: Cardinal Shuster of Milan (who is a candidate for sainthood, and whose body is incorrupt), Cardinal Segura of Toledo, and the Archbishop of St. John's, Newfoundland.

Two more years passed. On 4 September 1952, Fr. Feeney received a letter from Archbishop Cushing commanding him to appear at Cushing's residence to make submission. Then followed this warning:

> By direction of the same Sacred Congregation [the Holy Office], again with the full approval of the Holy Father, you are also warned to desist immediately from your activities as leader of the St. Benedict Center movement, under threat of still graver punishments to be determined by the Sacred Congregation.

The more attentive of my readers will note that the threats contained in this message were based upon the Holy Office letter issued three years and one day prior, yet never up to that time made public. Since Fr. Feeney and the Centerites had thus not read it, they could certainly not be expected to comply with it. But two days later, its signatory Cardinal having died, the letter was at last published in the *Pilot*, and shortly thereafter in the *American Ecclesiastical Review*. As noted, though, it never was published in the *Acta Apostolicae Sedis*.

St. Benedict Center sent another letter to the Holy Father on 24 September 1952. This latest message accused Archbishop Cushing of heresy, and maintained that the Letter of the Holy Office was both heretical and canonically invalid, the latter because it was never published in the *Acta Apostolicae Sedis*, which publication alone confers official and binding character on a document (and even then, only so long as it meets the proper forms).

There came from the Holy Office a response signed by Joseph Cardinal Pizzardo and dated 25 October 1952. Addressed to Fr. Feeney, it read:

The Supreme Sacred Congregation of the Holy Office has been obliged repeatedly to make your teaching and conduct in the Church the object of its special care and attention, and recently, after having again carefully examined and calmly weighed all the evidence collected in your cause, it has found it necessary to bring this question to a conclusion.

However, His Holiness, Pope Pius XII, in His tender regard and paternal solicitude for the eternal welfare of souls committed to His supreme charge, has decreed that, before any other measure be carried into effect, you be summoned to Rome for a hearing. Therefore, in accordance with the express bidding and by the special authority of the Supreme Pontiff, you are hereby ordered to proceed to Rome forthwith and there to appear before the Authorities of the Supreme Sacred Congregation of the Holy Office as soon as possible.

Five days later Fr. Feeney replied:

This is the first official notification I have received of the existence of a cause, judicially cognizable, in which I am an interested party. Your letter not only informs me that such a cause exists but also that there is to be a hearing for its disposition. A hearing or trial presupposed some formal complaint or accusation which serves as a legal basis for the proceedings and which also informs the accused of the charge against him so that he can prepare to defend himself. Before I can participate in a trial I would like to know with more adequate particularity what I am to be tried for.

Wanted to know what the charges were and what kind of court he would face, did he? Sounds like a reasonable request to you, does it not, fearless readers? Maybe it is, the more so because it is required by Canon Law. But what good is Canon Law if it acts as an impediment to slithering? Cardinal Pizzardo fired back a 22 November answer:

Your letter of 30th October clearly shows that you are evading the issue, instead of obeying promptly the order which was given you in the name of His Holiness, as was clearly expressed in my letter of 25 October.
You are to come to Rome immediately where you will be informed of the charges lodged against you.

> I wish to inform you that if you do not present yourself at the Congregation of the Holy Office before 31 December this act of disobedience will be made public together with the canonical penalties.

Quite a piece, this. Frankly, it reminds your author more of a communication from the court of the Great Oz in Emerald City than from the Roman Curia, whose zeal for justice is supposed to be bound up with its zeal for souls.

At any rate, Fr. Feeney replied with a longer elaboration dated 2 December. Therein he called the Cardinal's attention to the canons upon which his previous requests for information were based: 1715 required a formal statement of charges against a defendant; 1723 rendered a non-canonical summons null; 1959 forbade penalties without a trial; 1842 and 1843 required that the defendant be informed both of the charges against him and the nature of the proceedings to which he had been summoned; and so on. He then respectfully requested answers to his questions.

The 9 January 1953 final reply of Cardinal Pizzardo was somewhat less than responsive.

> In reply to your letter of 2 December 1952 asking for further explanations, the Supreme Sacred Congregation of the Holy Office communicates to you herewith the orders received from His Holiness, that you are to present yourself to this Congregation before 31 January 1953, under pain of automatic excommunication in case of failure to present yourself personally on the date indicated. This decision of His Holiness has been made after the arrival of the latest documents from St. Benedict Center.

Needless to say, this letter was as uncanonical as the others had been. Worse, the communications from the Holy Office were leaked to the press by someone either in the Boston Archdiocese or in Rome, which crime, as Fr. Feeney noted in his 13 January reply, incurred automatic excommunication for the violator reserved to the Holy See. After citing several other canons, Fr. Feeney noted that,

> The Cardinals of the Supreme Sacred Congregation of the Holy Office, as the Inquisitors-General of the Holy Roman Church, are bound by the decree which the Fourth Lateran... Council applies to all proceedings before inquisitors. "The accused shall be informed of the charges preferred against him,

that an opportunity may be given him of defending himself. His accusers shall be made known to him, and he himself shall have a hearing before his judges."

It is rather ironic to reflect that when the Inquisition in the Middle Ages had both the power to torture defendants and to turn over unrepentant heretics to the secular arm for execution, it was so renowned for honesty and scrupulous adherence to the law that lay folk would have themselves tried by it in preference to the secular courts upon any pretext they could think of; but in our time, when its penalties have been reduced to purely ecclesiastical ones, its functionaries have been capable of this sort of skullduggery. Oh, well.

Faced with these shenanigans, Fr. Feeney did not go to Rome, not supposing that justice would be served there, or that any attempt would be made to abide by the canons. Whether or not this was a prudent choice is certainly open to question, but it is certain that all doctrinal questions would have been avoided, matters of discipline only be dealt with, and that very likely in a non-canonical manner. The outcome was predictable: on 16 February, a decree of excommunication against Fr. Feeney, dated three days earlier, appeared in the *Acta Apostolicae Sedis:*

> Since the priest Leonard Feeney, a resident of Boston (St. Benedict Center), who for a long time has been suspended from his priestly duties on account of grave disobedience of Church Authority, being unmoved by repeated warnings and threats of incurring excommunication *ipso facto*, has not submitted, the Most Eminent and Reverend Fathers, charged with safeguarding matters of faith and morals, in a Plenary Session held on Wednesday 4 February 1953, declared him excommunicated with all the effects of the law.
>
> On Thursday, 12 February 1953, Our Most Holy Lord Pius XII, by Divine Providence Pope, approved and confirmed the decree of the Most Eminent Fathers, and ordered that it be made a matter of public law.
>
> Given at Rome, at the Headquarters of the Holy Office, 13 February 1953. *(AAS, vol. XXXXV, p. 100)*

While this decree did indeed make it into the *Acta Apostolicae Sedis*, that was as far as its canonicity went. For it was signed only by a notary, one Marius Crovini, not by either Cardinal Pizzardo or the Pope himself, whose signatures alone could make such a decree valid; nor did it carry the seal of the Holy Office.

Even so, Fr. Feeney and his followers were treated as excommunicates for almost twenty years after this. The notion that "Fr. Feeney was excommunicated for holding that you have to be a Catholic to save your soul" entered American Catholic mythology and remains there even yet. It is commonly taught in Catholic schools. Yet in 1972 all censures were lifted from Fr. Feeney, and he was not asked to make a retraction of his beliefs. This implied (much to the annoyance of Liberal Catholic papers at the time who vociferously denounced this) that Fr. Feeney had been right, and his opponents heretical. But of course, in true clerical fashion, rather than making any kind of real decision, the whole thing was merely considered closed, and the authorities in the case merrily slithered along. Indeed, from the 1950s to the present, "Feeneyism" and "Feeneyite" have been used as buzzwords to dismiss both the traditional teaching and one rash enough to hold it in this age of freedom and liberation. If your author had not conducted an extensive research into American Church history on this whole subject, he might fear being tarred with the "Feeneyite" brush himself for not having included a ritual denunciation of the man in this chapter. But he knows no scholarly person would be so foolish in his regard.

One of the results of the Fr. Feeney case, however, was to make adherence to the Liberal teaching "Outside the Church there is no Salvation except for all those who mean well," appear to be a hallmark of loyalty to the Faith. So many an old orthodox warhorse found himself at one with Karl Rahner on this point, much to that cleric's amazement.

It were well to leave the last word on the Fr. Feeney case to Frank Sheed, who had been a friend of his when that was a popular thing to be, although he was no friend of Fr. Feeney's teaching:

> ...He [Father Feeney] was condemned but not answered. When Boniface VIII said in the bull *Unam Sanctam* that it was "altogether necessary for salvation for every human creature to be subject to the Roman Pontiff," he seemed to be saying not only what Father Feeney was condemned for saying, but what a vast number of yesterday's Catholics had grown up believing. Everybody would have been helped by a full-length discussion. (Frank Sheed, *The Church and I*, p. 166)

THE FAITH CONDEMNED

One thing that is certain is that Fr. Feeney's "excommunication" gave all and sundry *carte blanche* to deny publicly the Church's teaching, and even to ridicule historic figures who had uncontestably held it. A single example of this will suffice. Fr. James Brodrick, S.J., a contemporary of Fr. Feeney's who had made his literary career in the field of biography, published *St. Francis Xavier* in 1952. So soon after Fr. Feeney's being dealt with, it was necessary to administer some "healthy" admonishment to those interested in a Saint who had shared Fr. Feeney's beliefs on the matter. Here are a few quotes:

> [Referring to a letter of St. Francis Xavier's just quoted] That passage reveals one of the serious limitations of St. Francis as a preacher of Christian truth to non-Christians. In his dealings with sinners within the fold... he could be and was the very soul of pity and understanding... But a change came over him when his interlocutor happened to be a Moslem or Brahmin. He stiffened and fell back on the old slogan, "the Christians are right, the Pagans are wrong", which is perfectly true, but not the best way to win the attention or the sympathy of pagans. Not sober Catholic theology but an overwhelming prejudice bred in his Spanish bones dictated his hard answer to the Moslem doctor, who was so plainly an earnest searcher after God... The mercy of Christ our Lord is not limited by the Seven Sacraments which He instituted to be the normal channels of sanctifying grace. He can produce in men's souls the effects of the Sacraments without the Sacraments, and may have seventy times seven other and secret channels to bring His salvation to millions of human beings who worship Him as the unknown God and believe in His justice. Contrary to civil codes, the code of the Catholic Church declares that ignorance of the law, provided it be inculpable ignorance, is a complete excuse for the law-breaker. The law in the present case is that outside the Apostolic Roman Church no one can be saved, "but it is to be maintained as equally certain that those who are invincibly ignorant of the true religion are in no way held accountable for

this in the eyes of the Lord" (Pius IX). St. Francis Xavier appears to have overlooked that second principle in his overwhelming concern with the first, but it may be taken to condone his harsh pronouncement at Malindi, for he was as much and as invincibly ignorant of Islamic theology and piety as any Moslem ever was of Catholic theology and piety. (pp. 108-110).

This is most astonishingly wonderful! St. Francis Xavier's wholly traditional and extremely effective apostolate (recall the 3,000,000 he baptized himself) was "not the best way", was it? Has any modern Jesuit done better? The appeal to anti-Spanish prejudices on the part of Brodrick's readers is touching indeed, to say nothing of the good Jesuit's voiding of the Sacramental system and debasing of Revelation (which must indeed be a lie, if it is not merely shot through with exceptions, but void entirely for the majority of mankind). Then he makes the question of Salvation a problem for Canon Law, and is bothered that St. Francis ignored an innovation which lay several centuries in the future. The last sentence is perversely insulting. But let us continue:

> [In reference to one of the Saint's condemnation of the Brahmin caste's practice] After that explosion, who will say that St. Francis was not a man of temper and spirit, as well as woefully inadequate views about Indian religion and civilization? For him, the old slogan always seemed to suffice, the Christians are right, the pagans are wrong, which, while being perfectly true, by no means precludes the existence of partial, fragmentary truth, of deep spirituality, of genuine holiness, in such a non-Christian religion as Brahmanism (p. 148). Still, all allowances made for Francis, it is impossible not to feel a little sorry for the Brahmins whom he trounced so mercilessly. For one thing, it was their country, not his, and the religion which they professed and served had a title to some respect from a foreigner, if only by reason of its venerable antiquity, so much more impressive even than that of the Holy Catholic Church. Besides, it has a metaphysic, a philosophy of being, as profound in its own way as any of which the Western world can boast, but of that St. Francis was completely ignorant... Even the idolatry which is not so theologically absurd as he imagined... (p. 149)

In all this we are far from the command of Christ to preach the Gospel unto all nations, and from the practice of that commanded by Apostles, Fathers, Doctors, Popes, Councils, and all the Saints. Indeed, it seems that the only reason a missionary should leave his own land is to pick up virtue and wisdom from non-Christians—which is precisely the message delivered by so many Catholic Missionary publications today. But we will allow Fr. Brodrick one last quote, in reference to another letter of St. Francis Xavier on Indian barbarism:

> That dreadfully summary judgment of India and Indians calls for a word of comment. It proceeded from the ignorance of Francis and closely resembles such famous foreign pronouncements as that England is a nation of shopkeepers, or Ireland a country of bog-trotters, or America a confederation of gangsters and Hollywood divorcees, or Spain a geographical expression inhabited exclusively by fascist vermin. St. Francis knew next to nothing of the real India, no more than did any of his European contemporaries. Rabindranath Tagore said with great justice that "the West did not send its heart to conquer the man of the East, but only its machine." St. Francis assuredly brought his heart, but the machine was there first and got in his way. The mystery and majesty of India eluded him altogether. He, the man of uttermost prayer, never guessed that he was in the most religious land in the world, a land which had taught countless millions of men to pray, Chinese and Japanese no less than Hindus. How tawdry and insignificant the brief histories and imperial ambitions of Spain, Portugal, France, Holland, and England appear when set over against India's three thousand years of ceaseless, passionate search for the eternal and the divine. The gross superstitions and popular idolatry which St. Francis witnessed are not, as he seemed to think, the whole of the story but its least significant part and, all aberrations considered, it remains true of India, as it was of Francis himself, that God is its entire adventure. (326-327)

Such a preposterous passage betrays a lack of belief in the objectively salvific nature of the Church, and a hatred of that Western Civilization which the Faith produced (to say nothing of an incredibly naïve view of Indian history). It was the great failure of the colonial Empires to export European heresy and unbelief as well as true Christianity to the third world; but St. Francis was not a typical example of Western failure as Brodrick assumes. Rather, he was a sign and portent of what true Western victory would have required and resulted in. At any rate, these passages are useful in understanding the views of "mainstream" Catholic theologians on the eve of the Vatican II Council: Brodrick was not, after all, considered radical. It is now time for us to consider the post-War career of Fr. Brodrick's and Fr. Feeney's fellow Jesuit, Karl Rahner.

We have met with Fr. Rahner here and there already, which is just as well, because he was the most influential theologian of our time. But Rahner, after all, was the culminating figure of a long process.

You will recall, most noble readers, our discussion of the problem of the Universals earlier. Since the time of St. Thomas, there has been a steady decay in belief in the reality of these Universals, upon which so much of the doctrinal integrity of Catholicism rests. Oh, some of the Platonic Humanists of the 15th and 16th Centuries such as Reuchlin, Pico Della Mirandola, Cardinal Bessarion, and Nicholas of Cusa fought against this trend, as did Romantics like von Baader and Goerres and the neo-Augustinian Gratry. Official Thomism also attempted to halt the process at an arbitrarily fixed stage. But this is not the way things happen; rivers flow unless diverted at their source.

In time, as Nominalism (which taught, you may recall, that the Universals are mere names) became triumphant after the Reformation, the very concept of the Universals came to be abandoned outside the Church. Within, of course, it was retained only in its maimed Moderate Realist sense. But what was the result of this? Some philosophers took refuge in complete materialism, denying the objective reality of the unseen; others in a total idealism, which denied the objective reality of sensual perception; and others at last in a skepticism which denied our ability to know anything about anything either way. In a word, Nominalism led to the negation and removal of philosophy from practical considerations for the most part. Modern philosophers to a great degree prefer to play with the definition of terms, rather than to explore truth. It was inevitable, given the intellectual poverty of Neo-Thomism, that clerics would turn to non-Catholic theories for their philosophical fulfillment—particularly since Ultra-Realism was so completely "discredited" by "authoritative" sources.

It is difficult to make hard and fast statements about modern philosophy, because it is so nebulous. But to understand modern theology it is essential to get some grasp of the topic, particularly with regard to Existentialism and Phenomenology. Neither is really a philosophy as such: the former is an attitude which opposes both "ideological constructions" (that is, the idea that any given doctrine known to man could be objectively true) in philosophy and rejection of philosophy as such (though your author, under the circumstances cannot understand why they bother). Phenomenology "concentrates our attention on the data of our consciousness in order to discover their object-relatedness." It opposes both the notion that all knowledge can be reduced to sense experience, and the one which "reaches things as they are outside of the knowing subject." Merging these two themes together produced the thought (if it can be so called) of Martin Heidegger (1889-1976).

Heidegger, an apostate Catholic seminarian, is a hard philosopher to fathom. In common with many modern philosophers, he made up words to express his concepts—concepts your author struggles to comprehend, and often thinks are not worth the effort. This may be mere dullness or oafishness on his part, but he supposes that lengthy explanations as to why we can't really know anything anyway are not important. But one has struggled more successfully with this topic, the learned Fr. Teodoro de la Torre in his *Popular History of Philosophy* (p. 358), sums up Heidegger's teaching as laying

> ...a foundation on which to start the search for Being. This foundation is in Heidegger's opinion a phenomenology: it begins with our own [human existence as it is factual (that is, without explanation)], which is at our disposal, and which has in itself the thread of Being.

This question of Being is a major question for Heidegger. Fr. de la Torre explains its significance in Heideggarian thought thusly (*op. cit.*, 355):

> Philosophy cannot begin until one faces the question of Being... Such Being is not nominal being, as in the expression: 'The sky is blue' (this is the being of grammar); neither is Being equal to "entities" or specific instances of beings (this is the being of science); nor is Being an abstract concept common to all being (this is the being of Aristotelian metaphysic...). The Being of which Heidegger speaks is the ultimate ground in which all entities share, and in virtue of which they are all beings. The

ground of being is not confused with God: if God exists... he is an entity, not a being.

Here we are far from any question regarding the actual state of man and the universe. The Fall, Original Sin, Salvation, God Himself—none are knowable, because we do not know what knowledge or being is. It has been the fashion for many centuries to make fun of the Medieval scholastics' question "How many angels can dance on the head of a pin?" But this was indeed a legitimate question, regarding the properties of the subtle matter Ultra-Realists maintained was combined with Form in the makeup of pure spirits. The existence of subtle matter was denied by the Moderate Realists. As with all the other questions of Medieval philosophy, it did have an important point; but this sort of prattle about Being is simply ridiculous. The important questions of human existence can never be asked under Heidegger's system, let alone answered. Why then has your author taken up your time with such stuff? Because of the fame of some of Heidegger's students. Among the Liberal Protestants the most noted were Paul Tillich and Rudolph Bultmann. Heidegger's most well-known Catholic students were two; a young Pole named Karol Wojtyla, now Pope Saint John Paul II; the other was Karl Rahner.

Fr. Rahner first won renown in the theological-philosophical circles as a "Transcendental Thomist." This group was started by a Belgian, Jesuit, Joseph Marechal (1878-1944), and had among its best-known representatives Bernard Lonergan (1904-1984) and Emeric Coreth (b. 1919). Basically, it is an attempt to synthesize Thomism (or at least its name) with the sort of Modern Nominalism we have been examining. At face value, it could be said to be an attempt to "baptize" these ideas as St. Thomas attempted to do with Aristotle; in reality, it has served as a philosophical boost for Modernism, providing justification for treating all dogma as No Salvation Outside the Church has been treated. In this effort, Rahner was and is the master.

Through his editorship of a number of editions of Denzinger and of the widely used encyclopedia of theology, *Sacramentum Mundi*, to say nothing of his voluminous works (most notably the multi-volume *Theological Investigations*) Fr. Rahner was able to get his ideas into wide circulation both before and after the Council. There, his influence was paramount. What were his concepts of dogma and salvation? Vol. XIV of his aforementioned series, dealing with the Church, will do. Therein, he tells us of the efforts of himself and his allies to reinterpret dogma.

> Without it being thereby destroyed or having its meaning completely changed... will be underestimated only by those who are too entrapped in an old-fashioned mentality really to feel the present day insuperable pluralism at all, and who therefore find it easy to be "orthodox" ... The modern Catholic has to recognize and unreservedly to endure this pluralism in his awareness as it also implies a difference between his own faith and that of the Church. (p. 36)

Very good, Fr. Rahner! So we need not believe what the Church believes, because of pluralism! Oh, frabjous day, callooh, callay! Further, we must do this! Indeed, on the next page, the good Jesuit informs us that "...there is, in fact, a wholly justified attitude of indifference towards this or that particular doctrine of the Church." How about toward the pronouncements of her theologians? Or is that a personal attack? Your author professes himself sorry for his lapse into discourtesy. But Rahner goes on to say on p. 91 that "Cases may perfectly well arise in which a Catholic Christian has a right, and under certain circumstances, a moral duty, to depart from some official doctrine of the Church of this kind."

In a word, just as we cannot be sure that anything outside the Church (like the existence of the page in front of you) is true, neither can we be sure of anything within her either. But then, why are we bothering at all? That question of why is never addressed, however, so let us make it a little more limited in scope. Why was Fr. Feeney punished for defending traditional doctrine, and Fr. Rahner rewarded for denying it? Why was Fr. Mueller thrown to the wolves and the Paulists upheld? Why... no. These are embarrassing questions, and today embarrassment is much worse than falsehood. So let us hurry and see what Rahner says about Salvation.

On page 282, Fr. Rahner presents in his uniquely opaque style his theory of the "anonymous Christian," an individual:

> Who even though he is a non-Christian is justified through the grace of Christ and through a faith, hope, and love for God and mankind which are to be qualified as specifically Christian in a special sense, even though this triad, constituting the single way

to salvation and possession of salvation, is something of which they are not objectively aware in the sense of having consciously explicated their specifically Christian dimension to themselves. Merely in passing it may be remarked that we might actually apply the term "anonymous Christian" to every individual who, in virtue of God's universal will to save, and thereby in virtue of the "supernatural existential," is inescapably confronted with the offering of God's self-bestowal and is totally unable to escape from this situation. In other words, according to this terminology, absolutely every man is an "anonymous Christian."

In other words, man is saved not through Baptism, but through Birth. Well! All is well, in this best of all possible worlds. But what of the Church herself who provides such as Rahner with the dog-like adulation of lay folk and comfortable incomes free from the necessity of anything so vulgar as real work? (Your author does not consider this penning of passages like the above honest labor.) Never mind. What of the salvific role of the Church in Rahner's view, which is now that of a majority of Catholic theologians? Rahner claims that he can

> Trace a course of development from the optimism concerning salvation for unbaptized catechumens in Ambrose, through doctrine of the baptismus flaminis [baptism of the flame of the Holy Ghost] and the votum ecclesiae [Vow of the Church] in the Middle Ages and the Council of Trent, down to the explicit teaching of Pius XII to the effect that merely an implicit votum [vow[for the Church and baptism... (p. 283).

He continues:

> Whatever may be the course of this development, whatever theological grounds there may be for justifying it, it can at all events be said that at least since the Second Vatican Council there can no longer be doubt that the Catholic Church, as a matter of her conscious faith,... positively asserts that it is possible for the non-Christian to attain salvation, though at the same time it declares that such salvation is achieved in ways that are known to God alone. In a tacit but noteworthy correction to the officially received theology which had hitherto been more or less unanimous on this point, it was declared at the Second Vatican Council that atheists too are not excluded from this possibility of salvation... The only necessary condition which is recognized here

is faithfulness and obedience to the individuals own personal conscience. (pp. 283-284).

Fr. Rahner has the grace to admit, however, that "No truly theological demonstration of this thesis can be supplied here from scripture or tradition" (p. 283). Neither from Scripture, nor from Tradition, in a word, not from the whole of Revelation which Rahner in any case does not believe in. So none of this is part of Catholic doctrine. It is part of nothing in particular, saved the foaming at the mouth of the Hound of Hell. Yet it was imposed upon the Church at Vatican II with great ease, due in no small part to the basic agreement of Fr. Rahner and the Conservatives on this one point, an agreement that shocked even Fr. Rahner:

> This optimism concerning salvation appears to me one of the most noteworthy results of the Second Vatican Council. For when we consider the officially received theology concerning all these questions, which was more or less traditional right down to the Second Vatican Council, we can only wonder how few controversies arose during the Council with regard to these assertions of optimism concerning salvation, and wonder too at how little opposition was brought to bear on this point, how all this took place without any setting of the stage or any great stir even though this doctrine marked a far more decisive phase in the development of the Church's conscious awareness of her faith than, for instance, the doctrine of collegiality in the Church, the relationship between scripture and tradition, the acceptance of the new exegesis, etc. (p. 284).

Though they might argue or complain, the Conservatives, way down at the root were already in agreement with Fr. Rahner (being possessed as they were of the sorts of opinions expressed by Fr. Brodrick). It is not surprising that there was no resistance to the suppression of the hour of Prime in the Divine Office, during which on many Sundays of the year the "horrible" Creed of St. Athanasius had to be recited. This ancient Creed begins: "Whoever wishes to be saved must, before all other things, hold the Catholic Faith, which unless one preserves integral and inviolate, without doubt he will perish eternally." The Creed ends with this clear profession of the dogma, "This is the Catholic Faith, which unless one faithfully and firmly believes, he cannot be saved." The suppression of Prime obviated bishops and priests alike from having to say that more than once a year (on Trinity Sunday).

After the Council, references to the Church's traditional teaching were speedily removed from the liturgy and sacraments. Prayers which mentioned No Salvation Outside The Catholic Church were dropped from devotional books. The forceful Profession of Faith and Renunciation of Heresy and Schism required of converts was done away with. A revolution had been accomplished, and all signs of the old regime must be excised. So, in fact, it was done.

Prior to Vatican II, the American *Catholic Almanac* carried in its glossary an article entitled *No Salvation Outside the Church*, which quoted and misapplied Pius IX in the usual manner in order to explain that the doctrine did not mean what it said. But after Vatican II, this was replaced in subsequent editions with *Salvation Outside the Church*. Therein we read:

> The Second Vatican Council covered this subject summarily in the following manner
>
> "Those also can attain to salvation who through no fault of their own do not know the Gospel of Jesus Christ or His Church, yet sincerely seek God and, moved by grace, strive by their deeds to do his will as it is known to them through the dictates of conscience. Nor does Divine Providence deny the help necessary for salvation for those who, without blame on their part, have not yet arrived at an explicit knowledge of God, but who strive to live a good life, thanks to his grace. Whatever good or truth is found among them is looked upon by the Church as a preparation for the Gospel. She regards such qualities as given by him who enlightens all men so that they may finally have life" (*Dogmatic Constitution on the Church*, No. 16).

This highly ambiguous passage may be given an orthodox interpretation, that is that all men of good will may receive the true faith explicitly, or it may be read in accordance with Rahner's dictates. That the *Catholic Almanac* so intends it to be read may be seen by the change of title in the article; this is typical of most Catholic reference books today.

The most liberal interpretations of the Vatican II documents have everywhere prevailed since the Council, despite the valiant efforts of such as conservative Fr. Brian Harrison to attach to them an orthodox meaning. Since almost all subsequent (and non-solemn) Papal teaching (including the *Catechism of the Catholic Church*) inevitably refers back to Vatican II's documents, it partakes of the Council's ambiguities or worse. As an example, Paul VI, in his *Credo of the People of God* explicitly states:

> We believe that the Church is necessary for salvation, for Christ is the one mediator and way of salvation and he becomes present to us in his Body which is the Church, but the divine design of salvation embraces all men. Those indeed who are in ignorance of Christ's gospel and of his Church through no fault of their own, who search for God in sincerity of heart, and who, acting according to conscience, strive under the influence of grace to fulfill his will, belong to his people, even though in a way we cannot see, and can obtain eternal salvation. Their number is known only to God.

The first part of the first sentence repeats the infallible teachings of Paul's predecessors, however, the "but" in the middle sets up a false opposition between the earlier teachings and God's will that all men be saved, a truth equally as Infallible. To reconcile these two supposedly opposed truths, the Pope then goes on in what has become the customary manner. That this passage too may be made to bear an orthodox meaning if one tries very hard is obvious; but that is not the meaning which the normal reader will derive from it. Paul explicitly states in his prologue to his Credo (*op. cit.*, II, p. 387) that "it is not a strict dogmatic definition…" The casual observer might wonder, in that case, why he bothered with it at all, for it serves only to confuse things further—unless of course, one was cynical enough to think that the Pope did in fact hold the Rahnerite view, but knowing its conflict with Tradition, would not attempt to define it. We are forbidden to judge the Pope's intentions; we may only deal with the results of his actions.

The major religious text for Catholic High School students and for adult education in America was *Christ Among Us*, by the then Fr. Anthony Wilhelm, C.S.P. First published in 1967 by Paulist Press (ah, our old friends!), it has sold over 2,000,000 copies, although publication was switched to the secular firm of Harper and Row after the Vatican insisted Archbishop Gerety's imprimatur be removed a few years ago. Your author will now share with his readers its insights on the question of salvation:

> There are other ways of being united to God besides baptism. Most of the human race has never heard of or cannot believe in Christ of baptism. As the world population increases, Christians become proportionately less. The Christian life begun by baptism is becoming more and more the privilege and responsibility of a few. Most of humanity is united with God in other ways. (*op. cit.*, p. 199*)*
>
> Many men come to God in this way through other, non-Christian religions... So, too, one who cannot believe in a personal God, through no fault of his own, but is committed to following his conscience, receives God's grace presence... God lives within many...unbelievers, though they may oppose him or those who try to work for him. (p. 200).
>
> Theology has no complete answer as to how, or even whether anyone may be damned forever. (p. 289).

This heretical viewpoint, as even Rahner observed, has no basis in Revelation. It is therefore Catholic in no sense at all. Yet it is dominant in most sectors of the Church today. It is an error which has slithered all the way to the top, and carried in its train either denial or trivialization of all other dogmas. So complete is its hold that most Catholic commentary on earlier writers is informed by it, á la Brodrick. Your author cites as a case in point the edition of Ven. Walter Hilton quoted earlier, which, you may recall, records Hilton's opposition to the then novel notion that belief did not matter with regard to salvation. Translator M.L. Del Masto's footnotes on p. 350 to that section quoted are most revealing:

> 1. The position Hilton refutes here is now the orthodox one and goes under the name Baptism of Desire, though in his own time it was, at best, a probable opinion *[probable? Your author must beg leave to differ considering the weight of the quoted authorities in the earlier chapters of this book].*
>
> 2. The position Hilton adopts here is that of Medieval Orthodoxy; without Baptism, salvation was considered to be impossible, and Dante Alighieri was forced, on the strength of this view, to consign his Virgil, "the Father of my soul," to Hell in his *Commedia*—albeit reluctantly, because that virtuous pagan (and poetic genius) was unbaptized. By 1950, however, when the Jesuit Leonard Feeney preached a doctrine almost identical with the one Hilton presents here, he with all his followers, was formally excommunicated {sic} by the Roman Catholic Church for persisting in spreading this heretical doctrine.

This sums up what the Catholic scholarly and administrative establishment holds in the matter: what was true is now false, what was orthodox is now heresy. In a word, if one holds that the Church is necessary for salvation, he supposedly may be expelled from that Church—which expulsion, however, matters not in the least to his eternal salvation! That which was believed by Saints, Fathers, Doctors, and Councils is now a crime, and slithering errors are imposed upon the consciences of the Faithful. This we know to be true, because we are so assured by the generality of the clerics, particularly those of Episcopal or (more importantly) academic rank. "What have you to say to that, you author!" Thus might some readers reprove me. Your author has little to say in reply, save that he has described (as he promised, you will recall) how the teaching of Christ faded to the teaching of *Commonweal*, and that the whole thing seems a lot of rot to him, if truth be truth. But St. John Chrysostom sometime Patriarch of Constantinople, has something to say, and to such a personage your author relinquishes the floor:

> I do not speak rashly, but as I feel and think. I do not think that many priests are saved, but that those that perish are far more numerous. The reason is that the office requires a great soul. For there are many things to make a priest swerve from rectitude, and he requires great vigilance on every side. Do you not perceive how many qualities a bishop must have that he may be apt to teach; patient towards the wicked, firm and faithful in teaching the Word? How many difficulties herein.
>
> Moreover the loss of others is imputed to him. I need say no more. If but one dies without baptism, does it not entirely endanger his salvation? For the loss of one soul is so great an evil as no man can understand. If the salvation of one soul is of such importance that, for its sake, the Son of God became man and suffered so much, think of the penalty the loss of one soul will entail. (*Third Homily, Acts of the Apostles*, quoted in Catherine G. Clarke, *Gate of Heaven*, p. 38).

It really does not matter what the numerical majority, whether clerical or lay, says at any given time: the Church is indeed a Universal, existing really and truly in the mind of God. It does not matter either if we live in Rome in the time of Innocent III, with orthodoxy triumphant and the rites of the Church performed with scrupulous attention and splendor; or as a *kakure kirishtan*—"secret Christian" —in 1854 Japan, bereft of the priesthood and all the sacraments save baptism and marriage for two centuries. As long as one believes the traditional faith, has been baptized, and accepts the supremacy of the Pope, he is a Catholic, whatever his circumstances—indeed, whatever the dispositions (heretical, schismatic, or orthodox) of the clerics around him. If the situation permits, he may receive the sacraments from them; for his own sake, not for theirs. It is perhaps for this reason that God has permitted the Apostolic Succession to remain in various places outside the visible unity of the Church.

When, in the last century, the great Vladimir Soloviev approached the question of the schism between Eastern Orthodoxy and Catholicism, he maintained that the anti-Papal and Schismatic beliefs of most of the clergy and lay intellectuals of his time did not affect materially the masses of the Russian people. The "Orthodoxy" of the former was simply hatred of Rome, center of the Church (as Soloviev believed) and little else. But:

> The difficulty does not exist for those folk who are really orthodox in all good conscience and the simplicity of their heart. When questioned intelligently about their religion, they will tell you that to be Orthodox is to be baptized a Christian, to wear a cross or some holy image on your breast, to worship Christ, to pray to the Blessed Virgin most Immaculate and to all the saints represented by images and relics, to rest from work on all festivals and to fast in accordance with traditional custom, to venerate the sacred office of bishops and priests, and to participate in the holy sacraments and in divine worship. That is the true Orthodoxy of the Russian people... the Catholic [peoples have] precisely the same religious basis that we have. (*Russia and the Universal Church*, p. 47).

The truth of this statement was brought out to your author by an elderly Serbian woman he knows, who from childhood has always believed in the supremacy of the Pope and the existence of Purgatory (both strenuously denied by the Serbian Orthodox priests) by dint of paying no more attention to the liturgy than to the priests' sermons. Those, she always expected would be wrong.

Our priests were smart: they changed the liturgy as well, having hijacked the organs of power necessary to do so. But we must be Catholic despite them. The Church has a power of her own, which the parasites who infest her will never be able to completely extinguish. It is that power which has drawn converts like Graham Leonard to her; it is that same power which has inspired various High Church Anglicans and Lutherans to reinstitute various practices discarded since their separation from Rome (and among us, since Vatican II). By themselves these practices are not enough for salvation, but they have led many in the past and will surely lead many in the future into the fullness of truth. Young people may be seen flocking to Tridentine Masses (under various auspices) and Eastern-Rite Liturgies in droves drawn thither by the force of the Church's power upon their souls, conscious or not. Saint John Paul II, regardless of his feelings in the matter, regardless of his motivations, approved a wider use of the Tridentine Mass (yes, your author knows such permission was not necessary as Benedict XVI told us, but it helped many who were not so aware), and several religious foundations and monasteries which may play in the next few centuries the same role as did Cluny. There are some bishops (even a few younger ones) who attempt to remain loyal to the Church's authentic teachings and practices, however they may be hampered by faulty seminary training; the same is true of more priests. Then there are the Traditionalist organizations, complete with all their struggles and legal questions, which nevertheless provide the means of living a truly Catholic life in the midst of all confusion. Add to this the Conservative organizations, however restricted they may be by too fine distinctions: they nevertheless focus attention on doctrinal and moral problems making life just that much more difficult for wayward shepherds. Also, let us remember all those who keep close to the Old Faith as best they may in their devotions: the Rosary, the Sacred Heart, the Stations of the Cross, and so on; who cherish sacramentals, trying their best to ignore all that the Newchurch priests demand of them. Do not let us forget either those portions of the Third World from the heathen. Here then, is the Church in all her splendor, laboring (as once she did under the Arians), but far from dead. In the very struggle between herself and the heretics who oppress her, she moves and breathes, and has her life.

What of the slitherers, the spiritual pornocracy (now alas, often all-too-physical)? Those who, despite being in reality out of the Church continue to exercise their apparent positions of authority. They were indeed the salt of the earth, but have lost their savor; and are now good for just one thing. The force of their heretical logic is overwhelming; thus those who believe them (particularly younger ones) are leaving the Church in droves—and leaving such clerics with churches as empty as their collection plates. The time will come when all the property is sold, when there is neither money nor prestige to be had from the Church. Then, those few elderly pornocrats remaining will slither away, and the next battle—rebuilding what they have ruined—will begin. After all:

> There is in certain ancient things a trace
> Of some dim essence –
> More than form or weight;
> A tenuous aether, indeterminate,
> Yet linked with all the laws of time and space.
> A faint, veiled sign of continuities
> That outward eyes can never quite descry;
> Of locked dimensions harboring years gone by,
> And out of reach except for hidden keys
>
> -Howard Phillips Lovecraft

***

One thing to be born in mind is that denial of the dogma we have been discussing is a sin. So late as 1959, *My Divine Friend*, a Ukrainian Catholic Missal for Sundays and Holy Days (*The Redeemer's Voice*, Yorkton, Sask., Canada) included this among other transgressions in its "Examination of Conscience" for Confession:

> Have I betrayed the Catholic faith by saying, that all religions are equally good and that a man may choose a Church of his liking and still be saved?

Obviously, from all that has gone before, most of us must admit to this last sin.

It were well to conclude our consideration of the Church as Ark of Salvation with a final quotation from Balai, chorepiscopos, that is, vicar general so to speak, of the diocese of Aleppo, Syria during the early 400s. This was after the Arian heresy had been substantially defeated, yet before the Nestorian heresy sheared off Iran and Iraq, and before the Roman Empire in the West had fallen—in a word, during a short-lived period of peace. It is perhaps one of the sublimest descriptions of the Church and its function your author has ever read:

> If [God] left his dwelling and chose to live in the Church, it was to persuade us to abandon our homes and choose Paradise instead. God came to live among men that men might come into contact with God.
> Yours is the kingdom of Heaven, the house of God is ours; and building the house, the workmen merit the kingdom. There the priest offers bread in your name and you give your flock your body to eat.
> Where are you, lord? In Heaven.
> Where shall we expect to find you?
> Here in the sanctuary.
> Your heavens are too high for us, but the Church is within our reach and we can find you there.
> Your throne in Heaven rests on a bank of flame: who would dare approach it? But the God of all power lives also in bread: whoever will may approach and taste.
> (Church and Mulry, eds., The Macmillion Book of the Earliest Christian Prayers, p. 97)

Let him who will hear, hear.

AFTERWORD: TWENTY-FIVE YEARS LATER

A quarter century has come and gone since I first wrote this book, and much has changed. Yet the question asked herein remains intensely controverted. Of course, more and more seminarians and priests are asking, "how could the Church have changed her teaching on such a salient point as her necessity for the Salvation of Souls?" How indeed? As this author wrote in an article for Catholicism.org[3]:

* * *

Three generations of Catholics since then have been taught to believe that No Salvation Outside the Church—so far from being defined three times and repeated by Trent—is a heresy, for which the hapless Father Feeney was excommunicated. The practical result of this development in the life of the Church was noted by Pope Benedict XVI in an interview last year:

> There is no doubt that on this point we are faced with a profound evolution of dogma. While the fathers and theologians of the Middle Ages could still be of the opinion that, essentially, the whole human race had become Catholic and that paganism existed now only on the margins, the discovery of the New World at the beginning of the modern era radically changed perspectives. In the second half of the last century it has been fully affirmed the understanding that God cannot let go to perdition all the unbaptized and that even a purely natural happiness for them does not represent a real answer to the question of human existence. If it is true that the great missionaries of the 16th century were still convinced that those who are not baptized are forever lost — and this explains their missionary commitment — in the Catholic Church after the Second Vatican Council that conviction was finally abandoned.

---

[3] "The Four Wounds and Five Joys of the Modern Church", http://catholicism.org/five-wounds-five-joys-modern-church.html

From this came a deep double crisis. On the one hand this seems to remove any motivation for a future missionary commitment. Why should one try to convince the people to accept the Christian faith when they can be saved even without it? But also for Christians an issue emerged: the obligatory nature of the faith and its way of life began to seem uncertain and problematic. If there are those who can save themselves in other ways, it is not clear, in the final analysis, why the Christian himself is bound by the requirements of the Christian faith and its morals. If faith and salvation are no longer interdependent, faith itself becomes unmotivated.

The practical result of this occurrence is that most Catholics today are either Universalists or Neopelagians, in Pope Francis' pithy phrase. But as we may see by the *Catechism of the Catholic Church*, this tacit Universalism is to some degree enshrined in what many consider part of the Ordinary Magisterium:

VI. The Necessity of Baptism

1257 The Lord himself affirms that Baptism is necessary for salvation.59 He also commands his disciples to proclaim the Gospel to all nations and to baptize them.60 Baptism is necessary for salvation for those to whom the Gospel has been proclaimed and who have had the possibility of asking for this sacrament.61 The Church does not know of any means other than Baptism that assures entry into eternal beatitude; this is why she takes care not to neglect the mission she has received from the Lord to see that all who can be baptized are "reborn of water and the Spirit." God has bound salvation to the sacrament of Baptism, but he himself is not bound by his sacraments.

1258 The Church has always held the firm conviction that those who suffer death for the sake of the faith without having received Baptism are baptized by their death for and with Christ. This Baptism of blood, like the desire for Baptism, brings about the fruits of Baptism without being a sacrament.

1259 For catechumens who die before their Baptism, their explicit desire to receive it, together with repentance for their sins, and charity, assures them the salvation that they were not able to receive through the sacrament.

1260 "Since Christ died for all, and since all men are in fact called to one and the same destiny, which is divine, we must hold that the Holy Spirit offers to all the possibility of being made partakers, in a way known to God, of the Paschal mystery."62 Every man who is ignorant of the Gospel of Christ and of his

Church, but seeks the truth and does the will of God in accordance with his understanding of it, can be saved. It may be supposed that such persons would have desired Baptism explicitly if they had known its necessity.

1261 As regards children who have died without Baptism, the Church can only entrust them to the mercy of God, as she does in her funeral rites for them. Indeed, the great mercy of God who desires that all men should be saved, and Jesus' tenderness toward children which caused him to say: "Let the children come to me, do not hinder them,"63 allow us to hope that there is a way of salvation for children who have died without Baptism. All the more urgent is the Church's call not to prevent little children coming to Christ through the gift of holy Baptism.

59 Cf. ⇒ Jn 3:5[ETML:C/].
60 Cf. ⇒ Mt 28:19-20; cf. Council of Trent (1547) DS 1618; LG 14; AG 5.
61 Cf. ⇒ Mk 16:16.
62 GS 22 # 5; cf. LG 16; AG 7.
63 ⇒ Mk 10 14; cf. ⇒ 1 Tim 2:4.

One may then look at the Catechism of the Council of Trent on the same topic:

Necessity of Baptism

If the knowledge of what has been hitherto explained be, as it is, of highest importance to the faithful, it is no less important to them to learn that the law of Baptism, as established by our Lord, extends to all, so that unless they are regenerated to God through the grace of Baptism, be their parents Christians or infidels, they are born to eternal misery and destruction. Pastors, therefore, should often explain these words of the Gospel: Unless a man be born again of water and the Holy Ghost, he cannot enter into the kingdom of God.

Infant Baptism: Its Necessity

That this law extends not only to adults but also to infants and children, and that the Church has received this from Apostolic tradition, is confirmed by the unanimous teaching and authority of the Fathers.

While one is struck immediately by the difference of tone, a close reading will reveal what appear to be irreconcilable differences between the two texts. On one level, there is an easy answer; the Tridentine Catechism, since it simply repeats in this area the Infallible Canons of that Council on the matter, must be held to be of greater weight than the CCC, which is a composite work. As its own foreword says of the CCC, "Its principal sources are the Sacred Scriptures, the Fathers of the Church, the liturgy, and the Church's Magisterium" —although it will be noted that the last is lacking in this particular question. The caution presented in the Social Doctrine Compendium's foreword seems worth recalling here: "In studying this Compendium, it is good to keep in mind that the citations of Magisterial texts are taken from documents of differing authority. Alongside council documents and encyclicals there are also papal addresses and documents drafted by offices of the Holy See. As one knows, but it seems to bear repeating, the reader should be aware that different levels of teaching authority are involved." If indeed the two Catechisms differ on any point, it would seem obvious that Trent's is the more authoritative—for all that the CCC is so good in so many areas—not least of which is its attempt to give equal time to the methods and manners of life of the Eastern portions of the Catholic Church.

...Nevertheless, the CCC epitomises Pope Benedict's assertion. The results, beyond what he mentions are manifold. Business-like clerics and religious, who seem more like commercial executives than bearers of God's truth; the general lack of concern about either the gaining or losing souls in day-to-day life, and much else besides. Since the Salvation of Souls is THE reason for the Church's existence, deprived of that *raison d'etre*, all the Church's efforts are tremendously weakened—including those in the social sphere. Individual Catholics, clerical or lay, attempt to define for themselves a reason for the Church's existence or their own activities—be it as social workers, medical healers, maintainers of what are really museums, folklorists, carriers-on of culture, and the like.

...It is the apparent unreality of the Faith to a huge proportion of its members. For the millions of poorly catechised laymen around the globe, this is simply the result of decades of poor catechesis. But it is present too among the highest levels of theologians. So it is that we read in the International Theological Commission's 2007 document, *The Hope of Salvation For Infants Who Die Without Being Baptised* a very interesting thing. After giving a fine historical analysis of the development of the teaching of the Limbo of the Infants, the document's narrative suddenly switches gears, with the bald statement, "In the 20th century, however, theologians sought the right to imagine new solutions, including the possibility that Christ's full salvation reaches these infants." Indeed, on this topic and the entire question of Salvation, the document is a telling revelation of the mental gymnastics theologians in modern times have had to undergo to try to alter the meaning of defined definitions while being unable to change their words. One is reminded of Humpty Dumpty's assertion in Lewis Carroll's Through the Looking-Glass:

> 'When I use a word,' Humpty Dumpty said, in rather a scornful tone, 'it means just what I choose it to mean—neither more nor less.'
> 'The question is,' said Alice, 'whether you can make words mean so many different things.'
> 'The question is,' said Humpty Dumpty, 'which is to be master—that's all.

* * *

Without either impugning or even attempting to discern the motives of the theologians who indulge in such word-mastership, there can be no doubt of the practical effect: to reduce Catholic dogma from a description of objective reality to a strange looking-glass world that can be altered at and by an exercise of the will. That is, it becomes a fantasy, and not a particularly exciting one either."

A quarter of a century ago, the penalty for just asking the question was to be punished as a "Feeneyite." But as Frank Sheed observed of Fr. Feeney himself, "he was silenced, but never answered." Now that such as the Pope Emeritus are asking it, we may hope that those days are over. If, in this work, I have contributed to the answer, I shall be satisfied.

Charles A. Coulombe
Monrovia, California
Michaelmas 2017

BIBLIOGRAPHY

GENERAL

Catholic Encyclopedia, 1911 Edition
The Douay-Rheims Catholic Bible
Enchiridion Symbolorum, Denzinger (various editions)
Enchiridion Patristicum, Rouet de Journal, Herder, Fribourg, 1939
The Church Teaches, Jesuit Frs., Herder of St. Louis, 1955
Faith of the Early Fathers, Fr. Wm. Jurgens, Collegeville, 1979
Patrologia Graeca et Latina, Fr. J.P. Migne, Paris, 1883
The Apostolic Digest, Michael Malone, Irving TX, 1987
Papal Teachings, Solesmes Monks, Boston
Summa Theologica, St. Thomas Aquinas (various editions)

KEEP US FROM DESOLATION

Commonweal, 27 Sept. 1991

PHILOSOPHY IN THE EARLY CHURCH

Letters to Corinth, Pope St. Clement I, PL
Apologia I, St. Justin Martyr, PL
Vision, Similitudes, The Shepherd of Hermas, PL
Against Heresies, St. Irenaeus, PL
Fourth Eclogue, Virgil, Trans. C.D. Lewis, Anchor, NY, 1964
In Jesu Nave, In Josue, Exhortations to Martyrs, Origen, PG
To Autolycus, St. Theopilus of Antioch, PG
The Athanasian Creed, Denz. 39
The Roman Martyrology, Newman Press, Westminster, MD, 1961
De Mysteriis, St. Ambrose, PL

Ecclesiastical History of the English People, St. Bede, Dutton, NY, 1916

Barlaam and Josaphat, St. John Damascene, (Loeb Classics)

BAPTISM OF DESIRE?

History of the Catholic Church, II, F. Mourret, SS, Herder, St. Louis 1946

Oration on Valentinian, De Mysteriis, De Abraham, Exposition on Psalm 118, St. Ambrose, PL

City of God, On Baptism, De Vera Religione, On the Creed, To the People of Caesarea, On St. John, St. Augustine, PL

Faith of the Early Fathers, Wm Jurgens, Collegeville (Commentary) 1979

Pope St. Zozimus, Denzinger 102

Epistle XV, Pope St. Leo I,

ULTRA-REALISM AND THE MIDDLE AGES

Pope Pelagius II, Denz. 246

Constantinople IV, Denz. 1833

Letters of Gerbert (Pope Sylvester II) H.P. Lattin, Col. U Press, NY 1961

Apostolicam Sedem, Denz. 388

Pope Innocent III, Decr. III, (cf. *Cath Encyc.*) cf. Denz. 423 and 413

Life of St. Louis, de Joinville, trans. R. Hague, Sheed & Ward, NY, 1955

Sir Hugh of Tabarie in Aucassin et Nicolette, Mason, Dutton, NY, 1910

Chivalry, Leon Gautier, Dover Books, New York, 1965

The Song of Roland, Penguin Classics Trans. D.L. Sayers, London 1957

Parzifal, Vintage Books, New York, 1961

The Quest of the Holy Grail, Penguin Classics, London, 1969

Divine Comedy, Dante, Trans. Tozer, Oxford, 1904

The Stairway of Perfection, Ven. Walter Hilton, Trans. M.L. Del Masto,

Image Books, Garden City, 1979

History of Philosophy, Paul Glenn, B. Herder, 1944

Council of Vienne, Denz. 481
History of Philosophy, Alfred Weber, Trans. Thilly, Scribner, NY 1896
Inventing the Middle Ages, Norman F. Cantor, Wm. Morrow, NY, 1991

THE NEW PHILOSOPHY AND ST. THOMAS

Catholic Art & Culture, E.I. Watkin, Sheed and Ward, NY, 1944
How Brief a Candle, Fr. John Coony, Cociti Lake NM 1980
Saint Bonaventure, Ephrem Bettoni, trans., A. Gambatese, N D Press, 1964
Summa Th., III, q. 68, art. 3
The Holy Roman Empire, J., Viscount Bryce, MacMillan, London, 1913
Unam Sanctam, Denz 468
Exultate Deo, Denz 696
Cantate Domino, Denz 715

A NEW THEOLOGY FOR A NEW WORLD

Mexico, Catholic Encyclopedia X
Ven. Mary of Agreda, WPA Guide to New Mexico
St. Junipero Serra, *California Missions*, 1979, Roberts
Fr. De Smet, Catholic Encyclopedia
Religious Memoirs, Sir Henry Taylor, Bahamas, 1988
Prayer of St. Francis Xavier, *Raccolta*, 1915
Creed of St. Pius V, Denz 1000
Trent, Denz. 861, 833, 858, 787
Pope Gregory IX (d. 1241) Denz. 447
Roman Catechism, Bradley & Kevane, Daughters of St. Paul 1981

THE HOUND OF HELL

History of Medieval Philosophy, F. Copleston, SJ Harper Row, 1972
Bishop Butler, (Poem), Anthology of Irish Poetry

The Peasant of the Garonne, Jacques Maritain, Holt Rinehart, NY, 1968

Baptism, Catholic Encyclopedia II

Preaching of God's Word, 512, St. Alphonsus Ma. Ligouri, NY, 1928

Preparation for Death, 339, St. Alphonsus Ma. Ligouri, NY, 1928

Auctorem Fidei, Denz. 1526

The Sincere Christian, Archbishop George Hay, Herder, St. Louis, 1911

Franz von Baader, *Encyclopedia Brittanica*, 1911 Edition

Mary in our Christ-Life, Ven. Wm. J. Chaminade, Bruce, Milwaukee, 1961

Eucharistic Handbook, St. Peter Julian Eymard, Sentinel, NY 1948

St. John M. Vianney, in *The Apostolic Digest*

St. Anthony Mary Claret, in *The Apostolic Digest*

Summo iugiter studio, Pope Gregory XVI, Papal Teaching

Singulari Quadam, (Denz. 1647), Ven Pope Pius IX

Syllabus of Modern Errors, (Denz. 1700 ff.) Ven. Pope Pius IX

Cross Upon Cross, p. 214, Fr. Francis B. Thornton, Benziger, NY, 1955

Quanto Conficiamur, Denz. 1678

Papal Teachings: The Church, Solesmes, nos. 653 and 668

Rome and the Study of Scripture, p. 77, Benedict XV, St. Meinrad, 1943

Encyclical *Mortalium Animos*, cap. 11, Pope Pius XI

Pascendi Gregis, Denz. 2078, Pope St. Pius X

CATHOLICISM IN AMERICA

Church and State in Latin America, p. 144, J. Lloyd Mecham

Catechism of the Christian Religion, St. John N. Neumann

Small Catechism, Fr. Joseph Deharbe, 1968

Life of Orestes Brownson, Vol III, Henry Brownson, Detroit, 1900

Brownson's Quarterly Review, July, 1874

Familiar Explanation of Christian Doctrine, Rev. Michael Mueller

Questions and Answers on Salvation, Rev. Michael Mueller

The Catholic Dogma, Rev. Michael Mueller
From the Housetops, #31, 1988
The One True Church, Rev. Arnold Damen, S.J.
Papal Teachings: The Church, Solesmes, #761, Pope Benedict XV
Christ the Life of the Soul, Dom Columbia Marmion, OSB 1920
The Liturgical Year, VIII, Dom Prosper Gueranger, OSB 1870
Travels of St. Frances Xavier Cabrini, New York

ATTACK ON THE DOGMA INCREASES

Is there Salvation Outside the Church?, Fr. Bainvel, SJ, Herder, St. Louis (TAN), 1917
The Spirit of Catholicism, Fr. Karl Adam, MacMillan, NY, 1929
Mystici Corporis, (Denz. 2286) Pope Pius XII
Catholicism, Fr. Henri de Lubac, SJ, Sheed and Ward, 1964
Jacques Maritain (quoted in The Death of Christian Culture)
Cantate Domino, Denz. 714
The Death of Christian Culture, Dr. John Senior, Arlington House, 1978
Open Letter to Concerned Catholics, Archbishop Marcel Lefebvre, 1986
The Raccolta, 1930 Edition and the 1952 Edition

VEILED SIGN OF CONTINUITIES

From the Housetops, September, 1947, Sentimental Theology
The Loyolas and the Cabots, Catherine Clarke, Ravengate, 1950
Encyclical *Humani Generis*, Pope Pius XII
They Fought the Good Fight, Thomas Mary Sennott, Catholic Treasures, Monrovia CA, 1988
Acta Apostolicae Sedis, Vol. XXXXV
The Church and I, Frank Sheed, Doubleday, Garden City, 1974

THE FAITH CONDEMNED

Saint Francis Xavier, Fr. James Brodrick, SJ. Wicklow Press, NY, 1952

Popular History of Philosophy, Fr. Teodoro de la Torre, Houston

Pope John Paul II and the Catholic Restoration, Paul Johnson, Seabury Press, NY, 1981

Theological Investigations, vol. 14, Fr. Karl Rahner, SJ, Seabury, 1976

Catholic Almanac, Fr. Felician Foy, OFM, editor (annual), IN, 1968

Credo of the People of God, Pope Paul VI

Christ Among Us, (Fr.) Anthony Wilhelm (formerly CSP) Paulist, NY 1967

The Stairway of Perfection, Ven. Walter Hilton, trans. M.I. Del Masto

Gate of Heaven, Clarke, Ravengate, Cambridge, 1952

On the Acts, III, PG, St. John Chrysostum, Printed as a footnote in the Newman Press, Westminster, MD, trans. Of his *On the Priesthood.* 1943

Russia and the Universal Church, Vladimir Soloviev, Bruce, 1938

Fungi from Yuggoth—Poetry—H.P. Lovecraft, Arcam, Sauk City, WI

The Macmillan Book of the Earliest Christian Hymns, Balau, editors Church and Mulry, NY, 1988

Other books by Charles A. Coulombe:

Puritan's Empire

The White Cockade

Every Man Today Call Rome

Star-Spangled Crown

Vicars of Christ

The Pope's Legion

Made in the USA
Monee, IL
02 February 2021